THE "ORIGINAL POEMS"
AND OTHERS

By ANN and JANE TAYLOR
AND
ADELAIDE O'KEEFFE

PRINTED IN GREAT BRITAIN

"In books, or works, or healthful play,
Let my first years be past,
That I may give for every day
Some good account at last".—Watts

THE
"ORIGINAL
POEMS" AND
OTHERS
BY
ANN AND JANE
TAYLOR · AND
ADELAIDE · O'KEEFFE
EDITED · BY
E·V·LUCAS
WITH · ILLUSTRATIONS
BY
F · D · BEDFORD

3 PATERNOSTER BUILDINGS · E·C· LONDON 44 · VICTORIA · STREET · S·W·
WELLS · GARDNER · DARTON & C°

INTRODUCTION

I.

It was practically inevitable that Ann and Jane Taylor were to write, for writing was in the blood. Isaac Taylor (1730-1809), their grandfather, though not himself an author, was the friend of Richardson and Goldsmith, and an illustrator of books. He designed and engraved the illustrations for *Sir Charles Grandison*. Charles Taylor, their uncle, engraved many plates, translated the *Adventures of Telemachus* from the French of Fénélon, and revised Calmet's *Dictionary of the Bible*. Later in life their father and mother wrote too, but not until Ann and Jane's own literary work was practically done, Mr. Taylor producing *Scenes of British Wealth*, *Bunyan Explained to a Child*, and some fifteen other books; and Mrs. Taylor, *Advice to Mothers*, *The Family Mansion*, and half a dozen other books, and, with Jane, *Correspondence between a Mother and her daughter at School*. Their brother Isaac wrote, among more than twenty other books, *The Natural History of Enthusiasm;* their brother Jefferys wrote nearly twenty books : their nephew, the late Canon Isaac Taylor, the lexicographer, wrote ; their niece, Helen Taylor, wrote. It was almost impossible to be a Taylor and not write.

There is little to tell of the life of either of the principal authors of this volume. Ann was born at Islington. opposite the church, on January 30, 1782; Jane was born in Red Lion Street, Holborn, on September 23, 1783. In 1786, their father, Isaac Taylor, moved to a large house at Lavenham in Suffolk, where he engraved for Boydell's Bible and Shakespeare, made water-colour sketches and engravings of Suffolk architecture, and

v

h

Introduction

superintended the education of his family. In 1796 he moved to Colchester, to add the labours of an independent minister to those of his profession.

Very early Ann and Jane commenced author, having the habit, when still quite young, of walking up and down the Lavenham garden hand in hand, reciting their couplets in

Ann Taylor
(From a sketch by her father.)

unison; while Jane earned fame in the village for her dramatic gifts. In her sister Ann's words:

'I can remember that Jane was always the saucy, lively, entertaining little thing—the amusement and the favourite of all that knew her. At the baker's shop she used to be placed on the kneading-board, in order to recite, preach, narrate, to the great

Introduction

entertainment of his many visitors; and at Mr. Blackadder's she was the life and fun of the farmer's hearth Her plays, from the earliest that I can recollect, were deeply imaginative, and I think that in " Moll and Bet," " The Miss Parks," " The Nun Sisters,' " The Miss Bandboxes," and " Aunt and Niece," which, I believe, is the entire catalogue of them, she lived in a world wholly of her own creation, with as deep a feeling of reality as life itself could afford These amusements lasted from the age of three or four till ten or twelve About the latter time her favourite employment in playtime was whipping a top, during the successful spinning of which she composed tales and dramas, some of which she afterwards committed to paper '

None of these early efforts have been given to the world ; but a copy of Jane's verses apologizing when she was nine for the inferior quality of her collected work (due possibly to the demands made on her attention by the obstinacy of her top), is printed in *The Family Pen*

> To be a poetess I don't aspire ,
> From such a title humbly I retire
> But now and then a line I try to write ,
> Though bad they are—not worthy human sight.
>
> Sometimes into my hand I take a pen,
> Without the hope of aught but mere chagrin
> I scribble, then leave off in real despair,
> And make a blot in spite of all my care
>
> I laugh and talk, and preach a sermon well ,
> Go about begging, and your fortune tell
> As to my poetry, indeed 'tis all
> As good, and worse by far, than none at all
>
> Have patience yet I pray, peruse my book ,
> Although you smile when on it you do look
> I know that in't there s many a shocking failure,
> But that forgive— the author is
>
> Jane Taylor

Furthermore, when she was ten, Jane Taylor thus appealed to her father for a piece of land for her own cultivation

> Ah, dear papa ! did you but know
>   The trouble of your Jane,
> I'm sure you would relieve me now,
>   And ease me of my pain
>
> Although your garden is but small,
>   And more indeed you crave,—
> There's one small bit, not used at all,
>   And this I wish to have

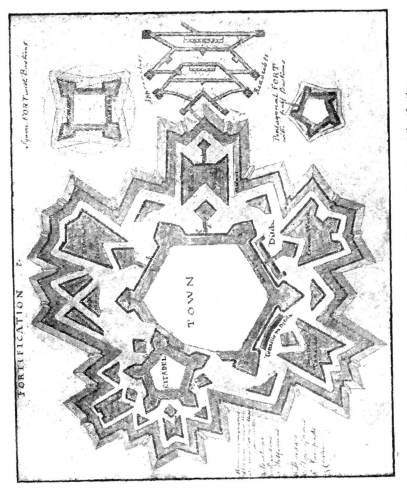

One of Isaac Taylor's plans from which his daughters learned fortification.

Introduction

A pretty garden I would make,
   That you would like, I know ;
Then pray, papa, for pity's sake,
   This bit of ground bestow.

For whether now I plant or sow,
   The chickens eat it all ,
I'd fain my sorrows let you know,
   But for the tears that fall

The picture of the two sisters, painted by their father, Isaac Taylor, in 1791, which is reproduced on page xi , shows Ann at the age of nine, and Jane twenty months younger. Mr Taylor's sketch-books are filled with portraits of his friends, his neighbours, and his family Among others is the round head of a sleeping and very placid baby in a frilled cap—his little son Isaac, born in 1787—against which has been written, ' The author of the *Natural History of Enthusiasm*.

In addition to ordinary home duties, Ann and her sister, both at Lavenham (1789-1795) and at Colchester (1795 and onwards), were learning engraving and drawing under their father, whose system of education was of a character so thorough that it comprised. even for his daughters, the principles of fortification Many of the *Original Poems* and *Rhymes for the Nursery* were written on the margin or on the back of maps of fortified towns, with such terms as ' glacis,' ' bastion,' ' circumvallation ' noted in the same hand. Indeed, so busy at their serious educational occupations were the two sisters that, their brother Isaac tells us, nearly all their work for the *Original Poems* and *Rhymes for the Nursery* was done in odd minutes snatched between more important tasks. Here Jane's early practice with her top must have served her in good stead Mr Henry Taylor, the nephew of Ann and Jane, whose house at Tunbridge Wells is filled with curious relics of the Ongar family, has a large collection of Isaac Taylor's educational drawings for his children, including several fortification charts, one of which I reproduce in small form on the opposite page Mr Taylor also possesses engravings by both the sisters : a little frontispiece by Jane to an edition of the *Hymns for Infant Minds*, and, by Ann, a scene of boors, after Teniers or Ostade or another of the jovial Dutchmen, engraved on copper with much skill and spirit.

Introduction

It must not be supposed, however, that the life of the little Taylors was all unrelieved strenuousness and military defence Their parents, though seriously minded and before all things instructive, had, I imagine, that pleasant intimate interest in whatever is interesting which might be called the noble part of inquisitiveness. Isaac Taylor was a very remarkable man, in many ways much in advance of his time. He left no subject where he found it, and invested with charm everything that he touched His drawings for the children illustrating the principles of mechanics are full of fun, and there is every indication that, though his published writings are somewhat severe and pietistic, his nature was genial and amusable. Mr. Henry Taylor permits me to print, probably for the first time, the following pleasant elegy from Isaac Taylor's pen on one of the Ongar cats :

EPITAPH ON A CAT

July, 1813

Here lies old Nut,
In pit-hole put,
    Death in his claws has got her
Her claws had tricks
Of pouncing chicks,
    And so the farmer shot her

Now do not sneer
At Pussy here,
    Nor scoffingly crow o'er her ,
Perhaps had you
Deservings due,
    You had been shot before her.

Of years fifteen,
Great age, I ween—
    Age e'en in cats we honour
But now to grow
So wicked, oh !
    This blasts her fame, fie on her !

Ah, had she died
By our fireside,
    When wintry rheums reduced her,
Her mistress's tears
Had crowned her years,
    Nor knave nor fool abused her

Ann and Jane Taylor, in the garden at Lavenham, in 1791.
(From a painting by their father, now in the National Portrait Gallery.)

Introduction

But cats are frail,
Yea, many a tale
  Of foolishness they give us :
Now should we say
'Twere not so,—pray
  Would anyone believe us ?

So, Puss, farewell
Thy tale I tell
  In verse, the long and short on 't
But who, and how,
Tell mine, I trow
  Is matter more important

A letter from Mrs Taylor at Colchester in 1804, when the rest of the family were in London, gives us a glimpse of the family at home in a mood of quiet fun. The dramatic scene is, of course, invented; it is Mrs Taylor's suggestion of what happened on the receipt of some mysterious chairs.

And now what *shall* I do to fill up my paper ? I can say I have just been called down to see Mr. Cecil, and every little helps, but as there is no particular news, I am still far behind I've a great mind to try my skill in ye drama way A writer must be a great fool indeed that cannot find an equal one for a reader, and so——

Scene   Angel Lane

Dramatis Personæ { Mr Isaac Taylor, sen   Miss Ann Taylor
Mr. Isaac Taylor, jun   Miss Jane Taylor
Mr. Martin Taylor

Children, Servant, and Porter

A ring at ye door.   *Servant enters*

SERVANT   There's a man with two armchairs
ALL.   Two armchairs ! ! !
SERVANT   Yes, sir, all done up in hay
MR TAYLOR   They can't be for us
ALL (*tumbling over one another*)   Let us see
ANN   They are for Taylor the dyer
JANE   But here is ye 'Rev '
ISAAC,   Oh, pay for 'em ! pay for 'em ! I daresay mamma has sent them from London
MARTIN   Yes, yes, that's likely I know mamma better than that You don't catch her at those tricks, besides, they are all gilt and japanned !
FATHER   Do hold your tongue, boy, and somebody pay for 'em, Who can lend me a shilling ?
ALL.   I've got none

Introduction

FATHER Can you change me a——? Call again Well, they are rare *easy* chairs, however, come they from whom they may They are such a support to one's back when one's tired

JANE. But if they should not be for us after all, we should look rare foolish

FATHER Ah, well, let's *enjoy* them while we have 'em, and not trouble ourselves who may sit in them to-morrow.

ISAAC Where will you set them, pa?

FATHER Why, I don't know, let them stand in the best parlour for ye present, to be safe from mischief, and mamma shall settle it when she comes home

JANE. Now, I'll lay anything I can tell where they came from You know Fowler's, a chairmaker, and he's very good-natured, and perhaps——   *[Curtain drops.*

A SHORT EPILOGUE

Wist ye not that such an one as *I*
Can certainly divine !*

Here we see not only where Ann and Jane (or Nancy and Jenny, as Mrs Taylor called them) found some of their impulse to write, but also perhaps why Jane as a child favoured the dramatic form.

Ann Taylor had made her first appearance in print in 1797, with (of all things) an election song. But that hardly counts Her true literary beginning was in 1799, when she was seventeen, with a rhymed answer to a puzzle in the *Minor's Pocket Book*. It was signed 'Clara' I have not seen it, this little annual being exceedingly rare. Jane's first printed poem was 'The Beggar Boy,' in the same periodical for 1804, when she was twenty. It ran thus.

I'M a poor little beggar, my mammy is dead,
My daddy is naughty, and gives me no bread
O'er London's wide streets all the day long I roam,
And when night comes on, I've got never a home

I would not be idle, like some wicked boys,
So I got me a basket with trinkets and toys,
Nobody was e'er more industrious than I,
Nobody more willing to sell if you'll buy

I've Buonaparte's life, and adventures, and birth,
And histories of all the great men of the earth,
Enigmas, and riddles, and stories complete
Come, buy them, dear ladies, a penny a sheet.

---

* The editor of Ann Taylor's autobiography adds that the chairs were a present from Mr Cecil, the mother alone being in the secret.

Introduction

Here's cottons, and bobbins, and laces so white,
And thimbles, and scissors, well polished and bright,
Fine pictures of Frenchmen, and Tartar, and Swede,
And Darton's gay books for good children to read

I've all the debates in the parliament made,
On sinecures, pensions, and taxes new laid.
Accounts of the battles by land and by sea,
That were fought in one thousand eight hundred and three

In summer, gay flowers and nosegays I sell,
Sweet cowslips, and roses, and jasmines to smell
Water-cresses for breakfast, fresh gathered and green,
From bad weeds and hemlock, picked careful and clean

But, alas! 'tis in vain that I mournfully cry,
And hold out my basket to all who pass by.
I fancy they're thinking of other affairs,
For they seem not to notice, or me or my wares

I would get me a place that was decent and clean,
Though in a capacity ever so mean,
But nobody credits a word that I say,
For they call me a vagrant, and turn me away.

In the evening I wander, all hungry and cold,
And the bright Christmas fires through the windows behold.
Ah, while the gay circles such comforts enjoy,
They think not of me, a poor perishing boy.

Oh, had I a coat, if 'twere ever so old,
This poor trembling body to screen from the cold,
Or a hat, from the weather to shelter my head,
Or an old pair of shoes, or a morsel of bread!

'Tis almost a fortnight since I've tasted meat,
Pray give a poor creature a mouthful to eat,
And while you in plenty all comforts enjoy,
Oh, think upon me, a poor perishing boy

II.

It was 'The Beggar Boy' which led to *Original Poems*.
The publishers of the *Minor's Pocket Book*, recognising the
merit of the verses, proposed to the sisters, who had already
done some engraving for them, that they should produce a
collection of poetry suitable for children. The kindly letter

Introduction

Isaac Taylor   London, *1st 6mo.*, 1803

Respected Friend
We have received some pieces of poetry from some branches
of thy family for the ' Minor's Pocket-Book,' and we beg that the
enclosed trifles may be divided among such as are most likely to be
pleased with them   My principal reason for writing now is to
request that when any of their harps be tuned, and their muse in
good humour, if they could give me some specimens of easy poetry
for young children, I would endeavour to make a suitable return in
cash, or in books   If something in the way of moral songs (though
not songs), or short tales turned into verse, or,—— but I need not
dictate   What would be most likely to please little minds must be
well known to every one of those who have written such pieces as
we have already seen from thy family   Such pieces as are short,
for little children, would be preferred
For self and partner, very respectfully,
Darton and Harvey

With extraordinary rapidity the sisters responded to the
publishers' invitation, for the first volume of *Original Poems for
Infant Minds* was ready in 1804, the second in 1805. According
to the title-page, ' several young persons' were implicated in the
work, but I cannot find particulars of any other associates than
Isaac Taylor, the father, who was not young (two pieces) , Isaac
Taylor, the brother (two pieces) ; Bernard Barton, the Quaker
poet, who was just twenty (one piece) and Adelaide O'Keeffe

Ann Taylor, in her *Autobiography*, gives the following
account of her sister's method of composition, which goes to
show that, young as she was, she had already divined the only
way in such an enterprise :

I have heard Jane say, when sitting down to our new evening's
business, ' I try to conjure up some child into my presence, address
her suitably, as well as I am able, and when I begin to flag, I say
to her, " There, love, now you may go " ' ̀

Adelaide O'Keeffe, who joined the Taylors in the composition
of the *Original Poems*, was the daughter of John O'Keeffe, the
dramatist, author of 'Wild Oats,' 'Modern Antiques,' and
scores of other merry farces and burlesques   Adelaide was born
in 1776, and was thus some years older than the Taylors. She
lived until 1855. Her contribution to *Original Poems* was thirty-
four pieces, some of which are amongst the most sprightly in the
volume   How she came to know the Taylors, and why she played

Introduction

so small a part in their subsequent lives, I have not discovered,
but from the circumstance that she produced over her own name
for a rival publishing firm a small volume of *Original Poems
Calculated to Improve the Mind of Youth and Allure it to Virtue*,
in 1808, and did not contribute to *Rhymes for the Nursery*, 1806,
we may suppose that some difficulty arose which separated the
old collaborators In 1848 Miss O'Keeffe put in a claim for a
further share of the profits on the original *Original Poems*,
but her demand was not well founded.

In addition to her 1808 *Original Poems*, from which I quote
in Appendix III, Miss O'Keeffe wrote several other books for
children, one of which was *Poems for Young Children*, 1848,
from which I also quote My object in including these verses
in this volume is twofold to provide some quaint reading,
amusing rather by accident, I fear, than by intention, and to
support a private theory that Miss O'Keeffe was a good deal
indebted to the Taylors for the excellence of her thirty-four
contributions to their book. Otherwise, how would her own
unassisted verses be so very naive and elementary?

It is sometimes stated that Jefferys Taylor, the younger
brother of Ann and Jane, contributed to the *Original Poems ,*
but this is hardly possible, since he was only twelve when the
book was published I have, however, included in Appendix IV.
four of his original fables from *Æsop in Rhyme*, 1820, in order
to show the fluency of his verse and the nature of his humour
His story, *Ralph Richards the Miser* (which is reprinted in *The
Family Pen*), proves him to have possessed gifts which, had
he abandoned juvenile literature and attempted something of
wider range, might have produced remarkable results. Like
his sister Jane, however, he seems to have been fatally restricted
by the desire to point a moral.

The *Original Poems* stand at this day in no need of com-
mendation, but it might be said that the secret of their longevity
and acceptableness is probably their simplicity and truth The
authors carefully chose their subjects from the daily life of
normal children (with a few heightened incidents, such as man-
traps, broken legs, fires, thrown in by way of spice) and not only
described them in language such as children would use, prettily
decked with rhyme, but also imagined them very much as a
child would have done Thus they naturally appeal to young
readers, while parents are pleased to feel so secure that the

Introduction

verses, while never sickly, steadily inculcate good morals and
manners, and quicken the gentler emotions. Great critics, as
well as those on the hearth, have found the Taylors' verses good
—among them Scott and Southey, Browning and Mr. Swinburne.

Of the three chief contributors to the book Ann was for the
most part the most serious and careful, Jane the most fanciful
and genuinely humorous, Adelaide the most dramatic, but each
was capable of trespassing upon the other's preserves, as when
Jane produces 'The Little Fisherman,' which is sheer Adelaide;
Adelaide breaks out into 'Rising in the Morning' and 'Going
to Bed at Night,' which are in Ann's own manner; and Ann
condescends to the robust humour of 'The Notorious Glutton.'

III.

It is a commonplace in literary criticism that once the way
is shown by an innovator there are a hundred imitators to
take it. Before the *Original Poems* were published, nursery
books, of which there were great numbers at that time, were
for the most part in prose. No sooner had the *Original Poems*
caught the taste of those who bought books for children than
similar collections began to pour from the press. All the writers
for children essayed verse ; and many of them (or their astute
publishers) shamelessly called their volumes 'Original Poems,'
with such a slight change in the sub-title as would save legal
proceedings—if in those early days legal proceedings were con-
templated or taken in the matter of children's literature.

The best of the Taylors' imitators was Mrs Elizabeth Turner,
author of *The Cowslip*, *The Daisy*, and other little books, which
have recently been reintroduced to the nursery, less, I fancy, to
correct its manners than to gratify the sense of fun or whimsi-
cality which the sceptical modern child has substituted for the
reverential awe and unquestioning belief in one's elders that
was common when the last century was in its infancy. In every
school of literature that is founded by a successful innovator
there are usually among the imitators and derivatives one
or two genuine writers who were merely waiting for some such
outside influence to incite them to give their native gift ex-
pression. Mrs. Elizabeth Turner was of these. It is possible
that she would have written none of her cautionary stories had
it not been for Jane Taylor's 'Little Fisherman' and Adelaide

Introduction

O'Keeffe's 'False Alarms'; but once these pieces gave her the
stimulus, she produced a large number of verses in the same
kind, a little lacking in the tenderness of her originals, but far
more ingenious in technique, and informed by a sense of drama
and pitiless fatality all her own.

Mrs Turner lives, if she may be said to live at all, by these
collections of stories alone, but the Taylors had another follower
whose name is among the greatest in English literature, although
his fame was won in other fields. In 1808 May Lamb, with
her brother Charles, set out to make for a rival publisher,
Mrs Godwin, two little volumes of *Poetry for Children*, which
should reap some of the harvest sown by the two little volumes
of *Original Poems* of 1804 and 1805. A very charming and
simple little collection was that which the Lambs made; but
the Taylors remained supreme.

Indeed, only twice was their supremacy assailed—once in
1807 09, when the world was full of the imitations of Roscoe's
Butterfly's Ball, and again in 1846, when Edward Lear's *Book
of Nonsense* came out to inaugurate a new variety of children's
verse, the chief exponent of which after Lear is Lewis Carroll.
But the fashion for the *Butterfly's Ball* type of narrative soon
perished, and Edward Lear and Lewis Carroll being (in this
connection) only writers of rhymed nonsense cannot be said
strictly to compete with the Taylors As writers of poetry for
children the Taylors have never been excelled or equalled

They occupy, indeed, a position peculiar in our literature.
Inspired children's books we have in some profusion, but the
Original Poems is the only one that I can call to mind which
was written immediately for children by authors who were from
first to last authors for children only. The *Pilgrim's Progress*
was to be a spiritual guide for adults; *Robinson Crusoe* was of
the nature of a literary hoax, *Gulliver's Travels* was to be a
savage commentary on the littleness of man (pleasant to think
of the trick played upon Swift by his genius ') , the *Tales from
Shakespeare* were the task work of a great humorist and his
sister; the *Book of Nonsense* was the play of a painter, and the
Alice books were the recreation of a mathematician Among the
children's books which have stood, and will stand, the test of
time, the *Original Poems* is, I believe, the only one of the
first order which was written for children by authors who were

Introduction

concerned only for the entertainment of little people. Hence
we must judge their work by a different standard than the
books which have become juvenile classics by accident Defoe,
Swift, Bunyan stumbled upon their nursery popularity; the
Taylors toiled for it Those wrote as well as they could for
adult readers, and pleased children too; these wrote only as
well as they could for children, deliberately excluding the grown
up intelligence I do not hold that had the Taylors written for
adults their works would still be read I think that exceedingly
improbable; but in considering the *Original Poems* we ought
to remember that the authors consciously worked only for tender
understandings

IV.

Between 1804 and 1810 Ann and Jane Taylor wrote other
books together, in addition to the two works reprinted in this
volume, chief of which was the *Hymns for Infant Minds*, 1808.
One of their joint volumes deserves particular attention, since
it represents a departure and shows us that both Ann and
Jane had in their earlier works exercised not a little repression
upon a tendency, observable continually in their brother Jefferys,
to satire In the *Original Poems* and *Rhymes for the Nursery*
the satirical mood was hardly fitting, but a few years later, in
1810, they had full opportunity to indulge it, having received the
commission to write for Tabart and Co *Signor Topsy-Turvy's
Wonderful Magic Lantern; or, The World Turned Upside Down*
—a little book that is now very rare The title-page of the copy
which Mr Henry Taylor has kindly lent me states somewhat
tactlessly that the work is 'by the author of "My Mother"';
but there is little of the spirit of that poem in it The *Magic
Lantern* was essentially a Taylorian undertaking, Ann and Jane
having provided the text—with assistance from 'T' (possibly
their brother Isaac, or even their father)—and Isaac Taylor
their brother having made the extremely clever and curious
drawings, worthy in spirit of the brain that devised *Gulliver's
Travels*. Indeed, the book has quite a Swiftian flavour, albeit
a little softened Its object was to fulfil that always unpopular
task—the exhibition of 'the other side' Throughout the work
the tables are turned a hare roasts a cook, a company of pigs

Introduction

stick a butcher, a fish drags an angler from the pool. Two horses thus discuss their possessions ·

'O yes, the fat farmer—an excellent breed !
I've purchas'd two capital fellows indeed
But I hear a prize farmer is soon to be shown,
That they tell me weighs upwards of seventy stone   ..'

'Why mine, tho' much leaner, are sad idle creatures,
They are such amazing extravagant eaters !
The pudding and meat they consume in a day,
Would keep my whole household in clover and hay '

This, by Ann Taylor, is one of the happiest of the pieces ·

THE FEATHER TURNED FINERY.

ONE morning an ostrich returning with glee,
    From laying her eggs in the sand,
Trotted under the boughs of a mulberry tree,
    Where a silk-worm was weaving her band

' Good day,' said the worm, wishing much to be heard,
    ' Any news in the papers, my dear ?'
' Who's there—is it you, my good friend ?' said the bird,
    ' Why, no, not a line that I hear

' Except—yes, I met with one comical thing,
    (Design'd, I suppose, for a skit),
An account of a feather I brush'd from my wing,
    Because it was ruffled and split

' And a cone of old silk you had dropt to the ground,
    (Choice articles both, I confess),
That one of those great human creatures had found,
    And made somehow into a dress

' And when it was finish'd (you wouldn t suppose
    Such queer unaccountable pride),
The creature imagin'd, because of its clothes,
    'Twas better than any beside !

' It walk'd to and fro for its fellows to see,
    And turn'd up its nose at the crowd,
As if it forgot, little cousin, that we
    Had really best right to be proud !"

' He ! he ! why, you don't tell me so,' said the worm,
    ' Ha ! ha !' said the bird, ' but I do,
But I keep you from dinner , good day to you, ma'am,
    Mind,—I don't tell the story for true.'

Introduction

The little book probably had a very small sale. It was Ann Taylor's last exercise in satire, but not Jane's, as we shall shortly see.

In 1810 Mr. Taylor left Colchester to become a Nonconformist minister at Ongar in Essex, where he remained for the rest of his life, until 1829. As it was at Ongar that his own and his wife's books were written, the family came to be known as the 'Taylors of Ongar'; but none of Ann's and only the last of Jane's works belonged to that village, although Ongar is probably pleased to claim them all.

In 1812, when Ann and Jane and their brother Isaac were at Ilfracombe, Ann received a letter from a stranger, the Rev. Joseph Gilbert, a Congregational minister (afterwards of Nottingham), saying that from her writings and from the report of her character which he had received from her friends, he desired to call upon her with a view to marriage. Ann complied with the romantic request, and they were married in the following year. Thenceforward, although, as I have said, she collaborated more than once with her sister, Ann Taylor, now Ann Gilbert, led her own life, brought up a large family, wrote a few religious books for children and a memoir of her husband, and died in 1866. Her Autobiography, containing many charming passages, was published in 1874. As a specimen of Mrs. Gilbert's pleasant manner I may quote her account of the relative importance of herself and her sister—surely a very difficult matter to handle with grace, and yet here done perfectly :

We were, perhaps, rather sought after as 'clever girls' at this time, and, of the two, Jane always conceding a large share of birthright to me, I seemed to be generally accepted as the cleverest. The mistake has been rectified by the public since, and, indeed, so as to swing a little beyond the mark, attributing to her many productions that are really mine. Publishers have frequently given a convenient wink, and announced 'by Jane Taylor,' when 'Ann Taylor' was the guilty person. Dear Jane never needed to steal, while I could not afford to lose.

Jane Taylor meanwhile was living with her brother Isaac (who afterwards wrote her life) at Ilfracombe, and later at Marazion in Cornwall, whither he was ordered for his health. Not until 1817 did she settle down at Ongar, where she interested herself in mission work, wrote her *Contributions of*

Introduction

Q. Q. for the *Youth's Magazine*, kept up a large correspondence, and nursed her failing health. She died at the early age of forty in 1824.

V.

Jane Taylor gave more promise than her sister of one day contributing to the adult literature of the nation. The *Contributions of Q. Q.* are often witty and always shrewd ; and her story *Display*, though impaired by its conscious purpose of instruction in good conduct—which now and then sinks it to the level of a tract—has many pages of very neatly turned comment not wholly free from malice. In this little book Jane Taylor the moralist is continually struggling for the mastery with Jane Taylor the quiz. It is better far when the quiz wins, as, for example, in the following passage describing one of Elizabeth's many attempts to do the correct thing :

Silhouette of Jane Taylor.

Mr. Leddenhurst was looking over a review.

'Poetry ! poetry in abundance for you, ladies,' said he, 'if you like it.'

'Oh, indeed, I am passionately fond of poetry,' said Elizabeth.

'Passionately fond, are you? Here is an article, then, that perhaps you will do us the favour to read.'

Elizabeth readily complied, for she was fond of reading aloud.

'We select the following passage,' said the injudicious critic, 'for the sake of three lines, which we are persuaded no reader of sensibility will peruse without tears.'

'No reader of sensibility !' thought Elizabeth ; 'but how should she discover for certain which they were in that long quotation ? To cry at the wrong place, she justly calculated, would be a worse mistake than not crying at the right ; but fortunately, as she approached the conclusion, the lines in question caught her eye, considerately printed in italics. She read them with great pathos, and as she read, tears—two undeniable tears—rolled deliberately

xxiii

her che   H   eeded in this nice hydraulic experi
down   she looked at her   and observed with some satisfaction
ment   on her cheeks there was no trace of tears   but glancing round
that   rest of the company she felt rather disconcerted to see how
at th   tly composed everybody was looking
perfe   re they not extremely affecting ' said she, appealing to Mr.
'A.   mhurst
Ledd

D   splay was written at Marazion in Cornwall in 1814-15,
          n its author was between thirty and thirty-two   The in-
wher   ce of another and a greater, though twelve-years younger,
fluer   is unmistakable   and though Miss Austen's delicate and
Jane   ltering irony was beyond the range and foreign to the
unfa   erament of her sister writer, there are not wanting signs
temp   had Miss Taylor lived and seriously attempted the novel of
that   ners, she might have written stories that would still be read
man   fter Display came the Essays in Rhyme on Morals and
A   iners   very skilful exercises in the art of Pope and Cowper
Mar   h more perhaps than any of her works indicate how
whic   ble was her mind   Here again, however, her didacticism
sens   quered, and, having the Moral Essays on the one hand and
conc   e Talk on the other, we find little or no room for the satirist
Tal   preacher of Marazon   Yet one of the little domestic satire
and   creation, stands alone   neither Pope nor Cowper had covered
'Re   t ground, nor has anyone since, so neatly is Jane Taylor
tha

RECREATION

We took our work and went you see
To take an early cup of tea
We did so now and then, to pay
The friendly debt, and so did they
Not that our friendship burnt so bright
That all the world could see the light
'Twas of the ordinary genus
And little love was lost between us
We loved I think about as true
As such near neighbours mostly do

At first, we all were somewhat dry
Mamma felt cold, and so did I
Indeed that room sit where you will,
Has draught enough to turn a mill
I hope you're warm, says Mrs G
'O, quite so, says mamma says she
'I'll take my shawl off by and by
'This room is always warm,' says I

xxiv

Introduction

At last the tea came up, and so,
With that, our tongues began to go.
Now, in that house you're sure of knowing
The smallest scrap of news that's going,
We find it *there* the wisest way
To take some care of what we say

—Says she, ' there's dreadful doings still
In that affair about the *will* ;
For now the folks in Brewer's Street
Don't speak to *James's*, when they meet
Poor Mrs. *Sam* sits all alone,
And frets herself to skin and bone
For months she manag'd, she declares,
All the old gentleman's affairs ,
And always let him have his way,
And never left him night nor day ,
Waited and watch'd his every look,
And gave him every drop he took
Dear Mrs. *Sam*, it was too bad !
He might have left her all he had '

' Pray ma'am,' says I, ' has poor Miss A.
Been left as *handsome* as they say ?'
' My dear,' says she, ' 'tis no such thing,
She'd nothing but a mourning ring
But is it not *uncommon* mean
To wear that rusty bombazeen ?'
' She had,' says I, ' the very same
Three years ago, for what's his name ?'—
' The Duke of *Brunswick*,—very true,
And has not bought a thread of new,
I'm positive,' said Mrs G —
So then we laugh'd, and drank our tea

' So,' says mamma, ' I find it's true
What Captain P' intends to do ,
To hire that house, or else to buy—'
' Close to the tan-yard, ma'am,' says I ,
' Upon my word it's very strange,
I wish they may n't repent the change !'
' My dear,' says she, ' 'tis very well
You know, if *they* can bear the smell '

' Miss F,' says I, ' is said to be
A sweet young woman, is not she ?'
' O, excellent ! I hear,' she cried ,
' O, truly so !' mamma replied.
' How old should you suppose her, pray ?
She's older than she looks, they say.'
' Really,' says I, ' she seems to me
Not more than twenty-two or three.'

Introduction

' O, then you're wrong,' says Mrs G.
' Their upper servant told our *Jane*,
She'll not see twenty-nine again '
'Indeed, so old ! I wonder why
She does not marry, then,' says I
' So many thousands to bestow,
And such a beauty, too, you know '
' A beauty ! O, my dear Miss B
You must be joking now, says she ,
Her *figure's* rather pretty '——' Ah !
That's what I say,' replied mamma.

' Miss F ' says I, ' I've understood,
Spends all her time in doing good .
The people say her coming down
Is quite a blessing to the town.'
At that our hostess fetch'd a sigh,
And shook her head , and so, says I,
' It's very kind of her, I'm sure,
To be so generous to the poor '
' No doubt,' says she, ''tis very true :
Perhaps there may be *reasons* too —
You know some people like to pass
For *patrons* with the lower class '
  And here I break my story's thread,
Just to remark, that what she said,
Although I took the other part,
Went like a cordial to my heart

  Some innuendos more had pass'd,
Till out the scandal came at last
' Come, then, I'll tell you something more,'
Says she—' Eliza, shut the door —
I would not trust a creature here,
For all the world, but you, my dear
Perhaps it's false—I wish it may,
—But let it go no further, pray !'
' O,' says mamma, ' you need not fear,
We never mention what we hear.'
And so, we drew our chairs the nearer,
And whispering, lest the child should hear her
She told a tale, at least too *long*
To be repeated in a song ,
We, panting every breath between,
With curiosity and spleen
And how we did enjoy the sport !
And echo every faint report,
And answer every candid doubt,
And turn her motives inside out,
And holes in all her virtues pick,
Till we were sated, almost sick.

Introduction

—Thus having brought it to a close,
In great good-humour, we arose
Indeed, 'twas more than time to go,
Our boy had been an hour below
So, warmly pressing Mrs. G
To fix a day to come to tea,
We muffled up in cloke and plaid,
And trotted home behind the lad

And again in the person of Matilda, in 'Egotism' a too familiar type of selfishness has been set down as well as it might be in the space, by a sure hand

MATILDA's friend, as few besides had done,
(A patient, quiet, unpretending one),
Sits cheerful and unwearied day by day,
To hear, as usual, what she has to say
By long experience, now at length, she learns
To drop all reference to her own concerns,
Th' insipid ' dear !' or ' sure !' too well declares
Impatience in discussing those affairs,
And then, the eager tone and alter'd brow,
How much her own are dearer—so that now,
—Whether her heart be aching, or it swell
With some sweet hope, 'twould be a joy to tell—
She checks the inclination, to attend
To some new project of her eager friend
How she intends, as soon as winter's o'er,
To make a passage to the nursery door,
Enlarge the parlour where she loves to sit,
And have the Turkey carpet made to fit,
Or, how she means next spring to go to town,
And then to have her aunt and uncle down.
Or if more intellectual in her mood,
How she employs her hours of solitude,
Her plans, how much they fail, or how succeed,
What last she read, and what she means to read;
What time she rises, and what time retires,
And how her deeds fall short of her desires
All this is very well, perhaps you cry,
True, if her friend might whisper, ' so do I '

Whene'er from home *Matilda* has to go
With the same theme her letters overflow,
Sheet after sheet in rapid course she sends,
Brimful and cross'd, and written at both ends,
About her journey, visits, feelings, friends
Still, still the same !—or if her friend had cast
Down in a modest postscript in her last,

Introduction

Some line, which to transactions may refer,
Of vital consequence, perhaps to her,
Matilda in reply, just scrawls, you know
Along that slip on which the seal must go,
' I'm glad, or griev'd, to hear of so and so '

The little volume contains one poem of a different turn—
' The Squire's Pew '—in a genre which several authors nearer
our own day have attempted with distinction, notably, perhaps,
Frederick Locker. A touch more of grace, and it would have
been perfect, as it is, 'The Squire's Pew' is a very pleasing
poem

THE SQUIRE'S PEW.

A SLANTING ray of evening light
Shoots through the yellow pane,
It makes the faded crimson bright,
And gilds the fringe again
The window's gothic frame-work falls
In oblique shadow on the walls.

And since those trappings first were new,
How many a cloudless day,
To rob the velvet of its hue,
Has come and pass'd away !
How many a setting sun hath made
That curious lattice work of shade !

Crumbled beneath the hillock green
The cunning hand must be,
That carv'd this fretted door, I ween,
Acorn, and *fleur-de-lis*,
And now the worm hath done her part
In mimicking the chisel's art.

In days of yore (that now we call)
When James the First was king,
The courtly knight from yonder hall
His train did hither bring ,
All seated round in order due,
With broider'd suit and buckled shoe.

On damask cushions, set in fringe
All reverently they knelt
Prayer-books, with brazen hasp and hinge
In ancient English spelt,
Each holding in a lily hand,
Responsive at the priest's command.

Introduction

Now, streaming down the vaulted aisle,
　　The sunbeam, long and lone,
Illumes the characters awhile
　　Of their inscription stone ,
And there, in marble hard and cold,
The knight and all his train behold

Outstretch'd together, are express'd
　　He and my lady fair,
With hands uplifted on the breast,
　　In attitude of prayer ,
Long visag'd, clad in armour, he,—
With ruffled arm and bodice, she

Set forth, in order as they died,
　　The numerous offspring bend ,
Devoutly kneeling side by side,
　　As though they did intend
For past omissions to atone,
By saying endless prayers in stone.

Those mellow days are past and dim,
　　But generations new,
In regular descent from him,
　　Have fill'd the stately pew ,
And in the same succession, go
To occupy the vault below

And now the polish'd, modern squire,
　　And his gay train appear,
Who duly to the hall retire,
　　A season, every year,—
And fill the seats with belle and beau,
As 'twas so many years ago.

Perchance, all thoughtless as they tread
　　The hollow-sounding floor,
Of that dark house of kindred dead,
　　Which shall, as heretofore,
In turn, receive, to silent rest,
Another, and another guest,—

The feather'd hearse and sable train,
　　In all its wonted state,
Shall wind along the village lane,
　　And stand before the gate ;
Brought many a distant county through,
To join the final rendezvous.

Introduction

And when the race is swept away
   All to their dusty beds,
Still shall the mellow evening ray
   Shine gaily o'er their heads ;
While other faces, fresh and new,
Shall occupy the Squire's Pew.

VI.

The text of the *Original Poems* and the *Rhymes for the
Nursery* which has been followed in the present reprint, is that
of a late revision by Ann Taylor, then Mrs. Gilbert.　Mrs.
Gilbert having decided upon the changed form of the verses, it
seemed right to adhere to it ; but I am doubtful if in every case
her alterations were for the best, and, entertaining this feeling,
I have placed in the Notes at the end of the book a few of the
earlier versions of the poems, and have also placed in Appendix I.
several pieces that were omitted from the later editions of both
the *Original Poems* and *Rhymes for the Nursery*.

From an engraving by Jane Taylor, executed
about 1805.

CONTENTS

Contents

Contents

Contents

RHYMES FOR THE NURSERY

Contents

Contents

Contents

APPENDIX I

APPENDIX II

APPENDIX III

Contents

APPENDIX IV

FOUR OF THE ORIGINAL FABLES AT THE END OF '.ESOP IN RHYME' BY JEFFERYS TAYLOR

A FEW NOTES

ILLUSTRATIONS

Illustrations

xl

ORIGINAL

P O E M S,

FOR

INFANT MINDS,

BY SEVERAL YOUNG PERSONS.

---◆---

"In books, or works, or healthful play,
 Let my first years be past ;
That I may give for ev'ry day
 Some good account at last."——WATTS.

---◆---

LONDON:

PRINTED FOR DARTON AND HARVEY, NO. 55,
GRACECHURCH-STREET.

Sold also by T. CONDER, Bucklersbury.

1804.

c

Preface to the First Edition, 1804

IF a hearty affection for that interesting little race, the race of children, is any recommendation, the writers of the following pages are well recommended ; and if to have studied, in some degree, their capacities, habits, and wants, with a wish to adapt these simple verses to their real comprehension and probable improvement—if this has any further claim to the indulgence of the public, it is the last and greatest they attempt to make. The deficiency of the compositions as poetry is by no means a secret to their authors ; but it was thought desirable to abridge every poetic freedom and figure, and to dismiss even such words as, by being less familiar, might give, perhaps, a false idea to their little readers, or at least make a chasm in the chain of conception. Images, which to us are so familiar that we forget their imagery, may be insurmountable stumbling-blocks to children, who have but few literal ideas : and though it may be allowable to introduce a simple kind, which a little maternal attention will easily explain, and which may tend to excite a taste for natural and poetic beauty,

3

Preface to the First Edition

everything superfluous it has been a primary endeavour
to avoid.

To those parents into whose hands this little volume
may chance to fall, it is respectfully inscribed, and very
affectionately to that interesting little race—the race of
children.

ORIGINAL POEMS

(*From the Edition of* 1854)

A True Story

L ITTLE Ann and her mother were walking one
    day
Through London's wide city so fair,
And business obliged them to go by the way
    That led them through Cavendish Square.

And as they pass'd by the great house of a Lord,
    A beautiful chariot there came,
To take some most elegant ladies abroad,
    Who straightway got into the same.

The ladies in feathers and jewels were seen,
    The chariot was painted all o'er,
The footmen behind were in silver and green,
    The horses were prancing before.

Little Ann by her mother walk'd silent and sad,
    A tear trickled down from her eye,
Till her mother said, ' Ann, I should be very glad
    To know what it is makes you cry.'

' Mamma,' said the child, ' see that carriage so fair,
    All cover'd with varnish and gold,
Those ladies are riding so charmingly there,
    While we have to walk in the cold.

' You say GOD is kind to the folks that are good,
    But surely it cannot be true ;
Or else I am certain, almost, that He would
    Give such a fine carriage to you.'

Original Poems

'Look there, little girl,' said her mother, 'and see
  What stands at that very coach door ;
A poor ragged beggar, and listen how she
  A halfpenny tries to implore.

' All pale is her face, and deep sunk is her eye,
  Her hands look like skeleton's bones ;
She has got a few rags, just about her to tie,
  And her naked feet bleed on the stones.'

' Dear ladies,' she cries, and the tears trickle down,
  ' Relieve a poor beggar, I pray ;
I've wander'd all hungry about this wide town,
  And not ate a morsel to-day.

' My father and mother are long ago dead,
  My brother sails over the sea,
And I've scarcely a rag, or a morsel of bread,
  As plainly, I'm sure, you may see.

' A fever I caught, which was terribly bad,
  But no nurse or physic had I ;
An old dirty shed was the house that I had,
  And only on straw could I lie.

' And now that I'm better, yet feeble and faint,
  And famished, and naked, and cold,
I wander about with my grievous complaint,
  And seldom get aught but a scold.

' Some will not attend to my pitiful call,
  Some think me a vagabond cheat ;
And scarcely a creature relieves me, of all
  The thousands that traverse the street.

' Then ladies, dear ladies, your pity bestow :— '
  Just then a tall footman came round,
And asking the ladies which way they would go,
  The chariot turned off with a bound.

'*The chariot turned off with a bound.*'

A True Story

' Ah ! see, little girl,' then her mother replied
   ' How foolish those murmurs have been ;
You have but to look on the contrary side,
   To learn both your folly and sin.

' This poor little beggar is hungry and cold,
   No mother awaits her return ;
And while such an object as this you behold,
   Your heart should with gratitude burn.

' Your house and its comforts, your food and your
      friends,
   'Tis favour in God to confer ;
Have you any claim to the bounty He sends,
   Who makes you to differ from her ?

' A coach, and a footman, and gaudy attire,
   Give little true joy to the breast ;
To be good is the thing you should chiefly desire,
   And then leave to God all the rest.'

A. T.

Original Poems

The Bird's-Nest

NOW the sun rises bright and soars high in the air,
  The hedge-rows in blossoms are drest;
The sweet little birds to the meadows repair,
And pick up the moss and the lambs' wool and hair,
  To weave each her beautiful nest.

High up in some tree, far away from the town,
  Where they think naughty boys cannot creep,
They build it with twigs, and they line it with down,
And lay their neat eggs, speckled over with brown,
  And sit till the little ones peep.

Then come, little boy, shall we go to the wood,
  And climb up yon very tall tree
And while the old birds are gone out to get food,
Take down the warm nest and the chirruping brood,
  And divide them betwixt you and me?

Oh no; I am sure 'twould be cruel and bad,
  To take their poor nestlings away,
And after the toil and the trouble they've had,
When they think themselves safe, and are singing so
    glad,
  To spoil all their work for our play.

Suppose some great creature, a dozen yards high,
  Should stalk up at night to your bed,
And out of the window away with you fly,
Nor stop while you bid you dear parents good-bye,
  Nor care for a word that you said.

The Bird's-Nest

And take you, not one of your friends could tell where,
    And fasten you down with a chain;
And feed you with victuals you never could bear,
And hardly allow you to breathe the fresh air,
    Nor ever to come back again:

Oh! how for your dearest mamma would you sigh,
    And long to her bosom to run;
And try to break out of your prison, and cry,
And dread the huge monster, so cruel and sly,
    Who carried you off for his fun!

Then say, little boy, shall we climb the tall tree?
    Ah! no—but remember instead,
'Twould almost as cruel and terrible be,
As if such a monster to-night you should see,
    To snatch you away from your bed!

Then sleep, little innocents, sleep in your nest,
    To steal you I know would be wrong;
And when the next summer in green shall be drest,
And your merry music shall join with the rest,
    You'll pay us for all with a song.

Away to the woodlands we'll merrily hie,
    And sit by yon very tall tree;
And rejoice, as we hear your sweet carols on high,
With silken wings soaring amid the blue sky,
    That we left you to sing and be free.

                            A. T.

The Hand-Post

THE night was dark, the sun was hid
 Beneath the mountain grey,
And not a single star appeared
 To shoot a silver ray.

Across the heath the owlet flew,
 And screamed along the blast,
And onward, with a quickened step,
 Benighted Henry passed.

At intervals, amid the gloom,
 A flash of lightning played,
And showed the ruts with water filled,
 And the black hedge's shade.

Again in thickest darkness plunged,
 He groped his way to find;
And now he thought he spied beyond,
 A form of horrid kind.

In deadly white it upward rose,
 Of cloak or mantle bare,
And held its naked arms across,
 To catch him by the hair.

Poor Henry felt his blood run cold,
 At what before him stood,
Yet like a man did he resolve
 To do the best he could.

So calling all his courage up,
 He to the goblin went:
And eager, through the dismal gloom,
 His piercing eyes he bent.

12

'*Poor Henry felt his blood run cold,*
At what before him stood.'

The Hand-Post

But when he came well nigh the ghost
  That gave him such affright,
He clapped his hands upon his sides,
  And loudly laughed outright.

For there a friendly post he found,
  The stranger's road to mark ;
A pleasant sprite was this to see
  For Henry in the dark.

' Well done !' said he, ' one lesson wise,
  I've learned, beyond a doubt,—
Whatever frightens me again,
  I'll try to find it out.

' And when I hear an idle tale
  Of goblins and a ghost,
I'll tell of this, my lonely walk,
  And the tall white Hand-post.'

A. T.

Original Poems

Spring

SEE, see, how the ices are melting away,
   The rivers have burst from their chain !
The woods and the hedges with verdure look gay,
   And daisies enamel the plain.

The sun rises high, and shines warm o'er the dale,
   The orchards with blossoms are white ;
The voice of the woodlark is heard in the vale,
   And the cuckoo returns from her flight

Young lambs sport and frisk on the side of the hill ;
   The honey-bee wakes from her sleep ;
The turtle-dove opens her soft-cooing bill,
   And snowdrops and primroses peep.

All nature looks active, delightful, and gay,
   The creatures begin their employ ;
Ah ! let me not be less industrious than they,
   An idle, an indolent boy.

Now, while in the spring of my vigour and bloom,
   In the paths of fair learning I'll run ,
Nor let the best part of my being consume,
   With nothing of consequence done.

Thus, if to my lessons with care I attend,
   And store up the knowledge I gain,
When the winter of age shall upon me descend,
   'Twill cheer the dark season of pain.

A. T.

Summer

THE heat of the summer comes hastily on,
   The fruits are transparent and clear :
The buds and the blossoms of April are gone,
   And the deep-coloured cherries appear.

The blue sky above us is bright and serene,
   No cloud on its bosom remains ;
The woods, and the fields, and the hedges are green,
   And the hay-cocks smell sweet from the plains

Down far in the valley, where bubbles the spring,
   Which soft through the meadow-land glides,
The lads from the mountain the heavy sheep bring,
   And shear the warm coat from their sides.

Ah ! let me lie down in some shady retreat,
   Beside the meandering stream ;
For the sun darts abroad an unbearable heat,
   And burns with his overhead beam.

There, all the day idle, my limbs I'll extend,
   Fanned soft to delicious repose ;
While round me a thousand sweet odours ascend,
   From every gay wood-flower that blows.

But hark ! from the lowlands what sounds do I hear ?
   The voices of pleasure so gay !
The merry young haymakers cheerfully bear
   The heat of the hot summer's day.

While some with bright scythe singing shrill to the stone,
   The tall grass and buttercups mow,
Some spread it with forks, and by others 'tis thrown
   Into sweet-smelling cocks in a row.

17

D

Original Poems

Then since joy and glee with activity join,
    This moment to labour I'll rise ,
While the idle love best in the shade to recline,
    And waste precious time as it flies.

To waste precious time we can never recall,
    Is waste of the wickedest kind
One short day of life has more value than all
    The gold that in India they find.

Not diamonds that brilliantly beam in the mine,
    For time, precious time, should be given :
For gems can but make us look gaudy and fine,
    But time can prepare us for heaven.

A. T.

Autumn

THE sun is now rising above the old trees,
    His beams on the silver dew play,
The gossamer tenderly waves in the breeze,
    And the mists are fast rolling away.

Let us leave the warm bed, and the pillow of down,
    The morning fair bids us arise,
Little boy, for the shadows of midnight are flown,
    And the sunbeams peep into our eyes.

We'll pass by the garden that leads to the gate,
    But where is its gaiety now ?
The Michaelmas-daisy blows lonely and late,
    And the yellow leaf whirls from the bough.

Autumn

Last night the glad reapers their harvest-home sang,
  And stored the full garners with grain
The woods and the echoes with merry sounds rang,
  As they bore the last sheaf from the plain.

But hark ! from the woodlands the sound of a gun,
  The wounded bird flutters and dies ;
Where can be the pleasure, for nothing but fun,
  To shoot the poor thing as it flies ?

The timid hare, too, in fright and dismay,
  Runs swift through the brushwood and grass,
She turns and she winds to get out of their way,
  But the cruel dogs won't let her pass

Ah ! poor little partridge and pheasant and hare,
  I wish they would leave you to live !
For my part, I wonder how people can bear
  To see the distress that they give.

When Reynard at midnight steals down to the farm,
  And kills the poor chickens and cocks ;
Then rise, Father Goodman, there can be no harm
  In chasing a thief of a fox.

Or you, Mr. Butcher, and Fisherman, you
  May follow your trades, I must own :
So chimneys are swept, when they want it—but who
  Would sweep them for pleasure alone ?

If men would but think of the torture they give
  To creatures that cannot complain,
They surely would let the poor animals live,
  And not make a sport of their pain !

A. T.

Original Poems

Winter

BEHOLD the grey branches that stretch from
 the trees,
 Nor blossom nor verdure they wear!
They rattle and shake to the northerly breeze,
 And wave their long arms in the air.

The sun hides his face in a mantle of cloud,
 The roar of the ocean is heard,
The wind through the wood bellows hoarsely and loud,
 And overland sails the sea-bird.

Come in, little Charles, for the snow patters down,
 No paths in the garden remain
The streets and the houses are white in the town,
 And white are the fields and the plain.

Come in, little Charles, from the tempest of snow,
 'Tis dark, and the shutters we'll close ;
We'll put a fresh faggot to make the fire glow,
 Secure from the storm as it blows

But how many wretches, without house or home,
 Are wandering naked and pale ,
Obliged on the snow-covered common to roam,
 And pierced by the pitiless gale !

No house for their shelter, no victuals to eat,
 No bed for their limbs to repose :
Or a crust, dry and mouldy, the best of their meat,
 And their pillow—a pillow of snows!

Be thankful, my child, that it is not your lot
 To wander, or beg at the door,
A father, and mother, and home you have got,
 And yet you deserved them no more.

To a Butterfly on giving it Liberty

Be thankful, my child, and forget not to pay
  Your thanks to that Father above,
Who gives you so many more blessings than they,
  And crowns your whole life with His love.

A. T.

To a Butterfly on giving it Liberty

POOR harmless insect, thither fly,
  And life's short hour enjoy ;
'Tis all thou hast, and why should I
  That little all destroy ?

Why should my tyrant will suspend
  A life by wisdom given ;
Or sooner bid thy being end,
  Than was designed by Heaven ?

Lost to the joy that reason knows,
  Thy bosom, fair and frail,
Loves best to wander where the rose
  Perfumes the pleasant gale.

To bask upon the sunny bed,
  The damask flower to kiss ,
To rove along the bending shade,
  Is all thy little bliss.

Then flutter still thy silken wings,
  In rich embroidery drest ;
And sport upon the gale that flings
  Sweet odours from his vest.

A. T.

Original Poems

The Tempest

SEE, the dark vapour clouds the sky,
   The thunder rumbles round and round !
  The lightning's flash begins to fly ,
 Big drops come pattering on the ground :
The frightened birds, with ruffled wing,
Fly through the air, and cease to sing.

Now nearer rolls the mighty peal .
   Incessant thunder roars aloud ;
Tossed by the winds the tall oaks reel,
   The forkèd lightning breaks the cloud ;
Deep torrents drench the swimming plain,
And sheets of fire descend with rain.

'Tis GOD, who on the tempest rides,
   And with a word directs the storm ;
'Tis at His nod the wind subsides,
   Or heaps of heavy vapours form :
In fire and cloud He walks the sky,
And lets His stores of tempest fly.

Yet though beneath His power divine
   My life depends upon His care,
Each right endeavour shall be mine ;
   Of every danger I'll beware ;
Far from the metal bell-wire stand,
Nor on the door-lock keep my hand

When caught amidst the open field,
   I'll not seek shelter from a tree ,
Though forms the falling rain a shield,
   More dreadful might the lightning be :
Its tallest boughs might draw the fire,
And I, with sudden stroke, expire.

The Churchyard

They need not dread the stormy day,
　Or lightning flashing from the sky,
Who walk in wisdom's pleasant way,
　And always are prepared to die :
I know no other way to hear
The thunder roll without a fear.

A. T.

The Churchyard

THE moon rises bright in the east,
　　The stars with pure brilliancy shine ;
The songs of the woodlands have ceased ;
　And still is the low of the kine :
The men from their work on the hill
　Trudge' homeward with pitchfork and flail,
The buzz of the hamlet is still,
　And the bat flaps his wings in the gale.

And see from those darkly green trees
　Of cypress and holly and yew,
That wave their long arms in the breeze,
　The old village church is in view.
The owl, from her ivied retreat,
　Screams hoarse to the winds of the night ;
And the clock, with its solemn' repeat,
　Has tolled the departure of light.

My child, let us wander alone,
　When half the wide world is in bed,
And read the grey mouldering stone,
　That tells of the mouldering dead :

And let us remember it well,
   That we must as certainly die,
Must bid the sweet daylight farewell,
   Green earth, and the beautiful sky !

You are not so healthy and gay,
   So young, and so active, and bright,
That death cannot snatch you away,
   Or some dreadful accident smite.
Here lie both the young and tne old,
   Confined in the coffin so small,
The earth covers over them cold,
   The grave-worm devours them all.

In vain were the beauty and bloom
   That once o'er their bodies were spread ;
Now, still in the desolate tomb,
   Each rests his inanimate head.
Their fingers, so busy before,
   Shall silently crumble away,
Nor even a smile, any more,
   About the pale countenance play.

Then seek not, my child, as the best,
   The pleasures which shortly must fade ;
Let piety dwell in thy breast,
   And all of thy actions pervade :
And then, when beneath the green sod
   This active young body shall lie,
Thy soul shall ascend to its GOD,
   To live with the blest in the sky.

                 A. T.

Morning

AWAKE, little girl, it is time to arise,
  Come shake drowsy sleep from your eye;
The lark is now warbling his notes to the skies,
  And the sun is far mounted on high.

O come, for the fields with gay flowers abound,
  The dewdrop is quivering still,
The lowing herds graze in the pastures around,
  And the sheep-bell is heard from the hill.

O come, for the bee has flown out of his bed,
  Impatient his work to renew;
The spider is weaving her delicate thread,
  Which brilliantly glitters with dew.

O come, for the ant has crept out of her cell,
  And forth to her labour she goes;
She knows the true value of moments too well,
  To waste them in idle repose.

Awake, little sleeper, and do not despise
  Of insects instruction to ask;
From your pillow with good resolutions arise,
  And cheerfully go to your task

JANE.

25

Original Poems

Evening

LITTLE girl, it is time to retire to your rest,
   The sheep are put into the fold,
The linnet forsakes us, and flies to her nest,
   To shelter her young from the cold.

The owl has flown out of his lonely retreat,
   And screams through the tall shady trees ;
The nightingale takes on the hawthorn her seat,
   And sings to the soft dying breeze.

The sun appears now to have finished his race,
   And sinks once again to his rest ;
But though we no longer can see his bright face,
   He leaves a gold streak in the west.

Little girl, have you finished your daily employ
   With industry, patience, and care ?
If so, lay your head on your pillow with joy,
   And sleep away peacefully there.

The moon through your curtains shall cheerfully peep,
   Her silver beams rest on your eyes ,
And mild evening breezes shall fan you to sleep,
   Till bright morning bid you arise.

JANE.

'*Young Thomas was an idle lad*' (p. 29).

The Idle Boy

YOUNG Thomas was an idle lad,
　Who lounged about all day,
And though he many a lesson had,
　He minded nought but play.

He only cared for top and ball,
　Or marble, hoop, and kite;
But as for learning, that was all
　Neglected by him quite.

In vain his mother's watchful eye,
　In vain his master's care;
He followed vice and vanity,
　And even learnt to swear.

And think you, when he grew a man,
　He prospered in his ways?
No: wicked courses never can
　Bring good and happy days.

Without a shilling in his purse,
　Or cot to call his own,
Poor Thomas grew from bad to worse,
　And hardened as a stone.

And oh! it grieves me much to write
　His melancholy end;
Then let us leave the mournful sight,
　And thoughts of pity send.

But yet may this important truth
　Our daily thoughts engage,
That few who spend an idle youth
　Will see a happy age.

JANE

29

The Industrious Boy

IN a cottage upon the heath wild,
  That always was cleanly and nice,
Lived William, a good little child,
  Who minded his parents' advice.

'Tis true he loved marbles and kite,
  And peg-top, and nine-pins, and ball ;
But this I declare with delight,
  His book he loved better than all.

In active and useful employ,
  His young days were pleasantly spent ;
While innocent pleasure and joy
  A smile to his countenance lent.

Now see him to manhood arise,
  Still cheerfulness follows his way ;
For as he is prudent and wise,
  He also is happy and gay.

For riches his wife never sighed,
  Contented and happy was she ;
While William would sit by her side,
  With a sweet smiling babe on his knee.

His garden so fruitful and neat,
  His cot by the side of the green,
Crept over by jessamine sweet,
  Where peeped the low casement between.

These filled him with honest delight,
  Though many might view them with scorn,
He went to bed cheerful at night,
  And cheerfully woke in the morn

30

The Little Fisherman

But when he grew aged and grey,
    And found that life shortly would cease,
He calmly awaited the day,
    And closed his old eye-lids in peace.

Now this little tale was designed
    To be an example for me,
That still I may happiness find,
    Whatever my station may be.

JANE.

The Little Fisherman

THERE was a little fellow once,
    And Harry was his name,
And many a naughty trick had he,
    I tell it to his shame.

He minded not his friends' advice,
    But followed his own wishes ;
And one most cruel trick of his,
    Was that of catching fishes.

His father had a little pond,
    Where often Harry went ;
And there in this unfeeling sport,
    He many an evening spent.

One day he took his hook and bait
    And hurried to the pond,
And there began the cruel game,
    Of which he was so fond.

31

Original Poems

And many a little fish he caught,
  And pleased was he to look,
To see them writhe in agony,
  And struggle on the hook.

At last, when having caught enough,
  And also tired himself,
He hastened home, intending there
  To put them on a shelf.

But as he jumped to reach a dish,
  To put his fishes in,
A large meat-hook, that hung close by,
  Did catch him by the chin.

Poor Harry kicked, and called aloud,
  And screamed, and cried, and roared,
While from his wound the crimson blood
  In dreadful torrents poured.

The maids came running, frightened much,
  To see him hanging there,
And soon they took him from the hook,
  And set him in a chair.

The surgeon came and stopped the blood,
  And bound his aching head ;
And then they carried him up-stairs,
  And laid him on his bed.

Conviction darted on his mind,
  As groaning there he lay,
And with compunction then he thought
  About his cruel play.

' And oh !' said he, ' poor little fish,
  What tortures they have borne :
While I, well pleased, have stood to see
  Their tender bodies torn !

32

Old Age

'Though fishermen must earn their bread,
  And butchers too must slay,
That can be no excuse for me,
  Who do the same in play.

'And now I feel how great the smart,
  How terrible the pain !
I think, while I can feel myself,
  I will not fish again.'

JANE.

Old Age

WHO is this that comes tottering along,
  His footsteps are feeble and slow,
His beard has grown curling and long,
  And his hair is turned white as the snow.

He is falling quite into decay,
  Deep wrinkles have furrowed his cheek ,
He cannot be merry and gay,
  He is so exceedingly weak.

Little stranger, his name is Old Age,
  His journey will shortly be o'er .
He soon will leave life's busy stage,
  To sigh and be sorry no more.

Little stranger, though healthy and strong,
  You now are so merry and brave,
Like him you must totter ere long,
  Like him you must sink to the grave.

Original Poems

Those limbs, which so actively play,
   That face, beaming pleasure and mirth,
Like his must fall into decay,
   And moulder away in the earth.

Then, ere that dark season of night,
   When youth and its energies cease,
Oh! follow with zeal and delight
   Those paths which are pleasure and peace.

So triumph and hope shall be nigh,
   When failing and fainting for breath;
And a light will enkindle your eye,
   Ere it closes for ever in death.

JANE.

The Apple-tree

OLD John had an apple-tree, healthy and green,
   Which bore the best codlins that ever were seen,
   So juicy, so mellow, and red;
And when they were ripe, he disposed of his store,
To children or any who passed by his door,
   To buy him a morsel of bread.

Little Dick, his next neighbour, one often might see,
With longing eye viewing this fine apple-tree,
   And wishing a codlin might fall:
One day as he stood in the heat of the sun,
He began thinking whether he might not take one,
   And then he looked over the wall.

The Apple-Tree

And as he again cast his eye on the tree,
He said to himself, 'Oh, how nice they would be,
  So cool and refreshing to-day !
The tree is so full ; and one only I'll take,
And John cannot see if I give it a shake,
  And nobody is in the way.'

But stop, little boy, take your hand from the bough,
Remember, though John cannot see you just now,
  And no one to chide you is nigh,
There is One, who by night, just as well as by day,
Can see all you do, and can hear all you say,
  From His glorious throne in the sky.

O then, little boy, come away from the tree,
Lest tempted to this wicked act you should be :
  'Twere better to starve than to steal ;
For the great God, who even through darkness can look,
Writes down every crime we commit, in His book ;
  Nor forgets what we try to conceal.

JANE.

35

Original Poems

The Disappointment

IN tears to her mother poor Harriet came,
   Let us listen to hear what she says :
' O see, dear mamma, it is pouring with rain,
   We cannot go out in the chaise.

' All the week I have longed for this holiday so,
   And fancied the minutes were hours ;
And now that I'm dressed and all ready to go,
   Do look at those terrible showers !''

' I'm sorry, my dear,' her kind mother replied,
   ' The rain disappoints us to-day ;
But sorrow still more that you fret for a ride,
   In such an extravagant way.

' These slight disappointments are sent to prepare
   For what may hereafter befall ;
For seasons of *real* disappointment and care,
   Which commonly happen to all.

' For just like to-day with its holiday lost,
   Is life and its comforts at best :
Our pleasures are blighted, our purposes crossed,
   To teach us it is not our rest.

' And when those distresses and crosses appear,
   With which you may shortly be tried
You'll wonder that ever you wasted a tear
   On merely the loss of a ride.

'But though the world's pleasures are fleeting and
     vain,
   Religion is lasting and true ;
Real pleasure and peace in her paths you may gain,
   Nor will disappointment ensue.'

JANE.

36

The Shepherd Boy

UPON a mountain's grassy steep,
  Where moss and heather grew,
Young Colin wander'd with his sheep,
  And many a hardship knew.

No downy pillow for his head,
  No shelter'd home had he ;
The green grass was his only bed,
  Beneath some shady tree.

Dry bread and water from the spring
  Composed his temperate fare ·
Yet he a thankful heart could bring,
  Nor felt a murmur there.

Contented with his low estate,
  He often used to say—
He envied not the rich or great,
  More happy far than they.

While 'neath some spreading oak he stood,
  Beside his browsing flocks,
His soft pipe warbled through the wood,
  And echoed from the rocks.

An ancient castle on the plain,
  In silent grandeur stood,
Where dwelt Lord Henry, proud and vain,
  But not like Colin, good.

And oft his lands he wandered through,
  Or on the mountain's side ,
And with surprise and envy too,
  The humble Colin eyed.

Original Poems

'And why am I denied,' said he,
 'That cheerfulness and joy,
Which ever and anon I see
 In this poor shepherd boy?

'No wealth nor lands has he secure
 No titled honours high;
And yet, though destitute and poor,
 He seems more blest than I.'

But this Lord Henry did not know,
 That pleasure ne'er is found,
Where pride and passion overflow,
 And evil deeds abound.

Colin, though poor, was glad and gay,
 For he was good and kind;
While selfish passions every day
 Disturbed Lord Henry's mind.

Thus Colin had for his reward,
 Contentment with his lot;
More happy than this noble lord,
 Who sought but found it not.

JANE.

The Shepherd Boy.

The Robin

A WAY, pretty Robin, fly home to your nest,
    To make you my captive would please me the best,
And feed you with worms and with bread.
Your eyes are so sparkling, your feathers so soft,
Your little wings flutter so pretty aloft,
    And your breast is all covered with red.

But then, 'twould be cruel to keep you, I know,
So stretch out your wings, little Robin, and go,
    Fly home to your young ones again,
Go listen once more to your mate's pretty song,
And chirrup and twitter there all the day long,
    Secure from the wind and the rain.

But when the leaves fall, and the winter-winds blow,
And the green fields are covered all over with snow,
    And the clouds in white feathers descend;
When the springs are all ice, and the rivulets freeze,
And the long shining icicles drop from the trees,
    Then, Robin, remember your friend.

With cold and with hunger half-famished and weak,
Then tap at my window again with your beak,
    Nor shall your petition be vain:
You shall fly to my bosom and perch on my thumbs,
Or hop round the table, and pick up the crumbs,
    And need not be hungry again.

JANE.

Original Poems

The Child's Monitor

THE wind blows down the largest tree,
    And yet the wind I cannot see !
Playmates far off, who have been kind,
My thought can bring before my mind ;
The past by it is present brought,
And yet I cannot see my thought.
The charming rose scents all the air,
Yet I can see no perfume there.
Blithe Robin's notes how sweet, how clear !
From his small bill they reach my ear,
And whilst upon the air they float,
I hear, yet cannot see a note.
When I would do what is forbid,
By *something* in my heart I'm chid ;
When good, I think, then quick and pat,
That *something* says, ' My child, do that :'
When I too near the stream would go,
So pleased to see the waters flow,
That *something* says, without a sound,
' Take care, dear child, you may be drowned '
And for the poor whene'er I grieve,
That *something* says, ' A penny give.'

    Thus *something* very near must be,
Although invisible to me ,
Whate'er I do, it sees me still .
O then, good Spirit, guide my will.

ADELAIDE.

The Boys and the Apple-Tree

The Boys and the Apple-tree

AS William and Thomas were walking one day,
    They came by a fine orchard's side:
They would rather eat apples than spell, read, or play,
    And Thomas to William then cried:

'O brother, look yonder! what clusters hang there!
    I'll try and climb over the wall:
I must have an apple; I will have a pear;
    Although it should cost me a fall!'

Said William to Thomas, 'To steal is a sin,
    Mamma has oft told this to thee:
I never have stole, nor will I begin,
    So the apples may hang on the tree.'

'You are a good boy, as you ever have been,'
    Said Thomas, 'let's walk on, my lad ·
We'll call on our schoolfellow, Benjamin Green
    Who to see us, I know, will be glad.'

They came to the house, and asked at the gate,
    'Is Benjamin Green now at home?'
But Benjamin did not allow them to wait,
    And brought them both into the room

And he smiled, and he laughed, and capered with joy,
    His little companions to greet.
'And we too are happy,' said each little boy,
    'Our playfellow dear thus to meet.'

'Come, walk in our garden, this morning so fine,
    We may, for my father gives leave,
And more, he invites you to stay here and dine;
    And a most happy day we shall have!'

43

Original Poems

But when in the garden, they found 'twas the same
   They saw as they walked in the road;
And near the high wall, when those little boys came,
   They started, as if from a toad :—

'That large ring of iron, you see on the ground,
   With terrible teeth like a saw,'
Said their friend, 'the guard of our garden is found,
   And it keeps all intruders in awe.

'If any the warning without set at nought,
   Their legs then this man-trap must tear.'
Said William to Thomas, 'So you'd have been caught,
   If you had leap'd over just there.'

Cried Thomas, in terror of what now he saw,
   'With my faults I will heartily grapple ;
For I learn what may happen by breaking a law,
   Although but in stealing an apple.'

ADELAIDE.

' " So you'd have been caught,
If you had leap'd over just there."

The Wooden Doll and the Wax Doll

THERE were two friends, a very charming pair!
　　Brunette the brown, and Blanchidine the fair;
And she to love Brunette did constantly incline,
Nor less did Brunette love sweet Blanchidine.
Brunette in dress was neat, yet always plain;
But Blanchidine of finery was vain.
　　Now Blanchidine a new aquaintance made—
A little girl most sumptuously arrayed,
In plumes and ribbons, gaudy to behold,
And India frock, with spots of shining gold.
Said Blanchidine, 'A girl so richly dressed,
Should surely be by every one caressed.
To play with me if she will condescend,
Henceforth 'tis she alone shall be my friend.'
And so for this new friend, in silks adorned,
Her poor Brunette was slighted, left, and scorned.
　　Of Blanchidine's vast stock of pretty toys,
A wooden doll her every thought employs;
Its neck so white, so smooth, its cheeks so red—
She kissed, she fondled, and she took to bed
　　Mamma now brought her home a doll of wax,
Its hair in ringlets white, and soft as flax:
Its eyes could open and its eyes could shut,
And on it, too, with taste its clothes were put.
'My dear wax doll!' sweet Blanchidine would cry—
Her doll of wood was thrown neglected by.
　　One summer's day, 'twas in the month of June,
The sun blazed out in all the heat of noon:

47

Original Poems

' My waxen doll,' she cried, ' my dear, my charmer !
What, are you cold ? but you shall soon be warmer.'
She laid it in the sun—misfortune dire !
The wax ran down as if before the fire !
Each beauteous feature quickly disappeared,
And melting, left a blank all soiled and smeared.
Her doll disfigured, she beheld amazed,
And thus expressed her sorrow as she gazed :
' Is it for you my heart I have estranged
From that I fondly loved, which has not changed ?
Just so may change my new acquaintance fine,
For whom I left Brunette, that friend of mine.
No more by outside show will I be lured ;
Of such capricious whims I think I'm cured :
To plain old friends my heart shall still be true,
Nor change for every face because 'tis new.'
Her slighted wooden doll resumed its charms,
And wronged Brunette she clasped within her arms.

ADELAIDE.

'To plain old friends my heart shall still be true.'　F

Idle Richard and the Goat

JOHN Brown is a man without houses or lands ;
   Himself he supports by the work of his hands :
   He brings home his wages each Saturday night ;
To his wife and his children a very good sight.
   His eldest son, Richard, on errands when sent,
To loiter and chatter is very much bent ;
And in spite of the care his mother bestows,
He is known by his tatters wherever he goes.
His shoes too are worn, and his feet are half bare,
And now it is time he should have a new pair ;
'Go at once to the shop,' said John Brown to his son,
'And change me this bank-note—I have only one.'
But now comes the mischief, for Richard would stop
To prate with a boy at a green-grocer's shop !
And to whom in his boasting he shows his bank-note :
Just then to the green-stall up marches a goat.
The boys knew full well that it was this goat's way,
With any that passed her, to gambol and play :
The three then continued to skip and to frisk,
Till his note on some greens Dick happened to whisk :
And what was his wonder to see the rude goat,
In munching the greens, eat up his bank-note !
To his father he ran, in dismay, with the news,
And by stopping to gossip he lost his new shoes.

ADELAIDE.

51

Original Poems

Never play with Fire

MY prayers I said, I went to bed,
　　And quickly fell asleep;
But soon I woke, my sleep was broke—
　　I through my curtains peep.

I heard a noise of men and boys,
　　The watchman's rattle too;
And 'Fire!' they cry, and then cried I
　　'Alas! what shall I do?'

A shout so loud, came from the crowd,
　　Around, above, below,
And in the street the neighbours meet,
　　Who would the matter know.

Now down the stairs run threes and pairs,
　　Enough their bones to break;
The firemen shout, the engines spout
　　Their streams, the fire to slake

The roof and wall, the stairs and all,
　　And rafters tumble in .
Red flames and blaze, now all amaze,
　　And make a dreadful din!

And each one screams, when bricks and beams
　　Come tumbling on their heads,
And some are smashed, and some are dashed ,
　　Some leap on feather-beds.

Some burn, some choke with fire and smoke;
　　But ah ! what was the cause?
My heart's dismayed—last night I played
　　With Thomas, lighting straws!

　　　　　　　　　　　　　ADELAIDE.

The Truant Boys

THE month was August and the morning cool,
    When Hal and Ned,
To walk together to the neighbouring school,
    Rose early from their bed.

When near the school, Hal said, ' Why con your task,
    Demure and prim ?
Ere we go in, let me one question ask,
    Ned, shall we go and swim ?'

Fearless of future punishment or blame,
    Away they hied,
Through many a verdant field, until they came
    Unto the river's side.

The broad stream narrowed in its onward course,
    And deep and still
It silent ran, and yet with rapid force,
    To turn a neighbouring mill

Under the mill an arch gaped wide, and seemed
    The jaws of death !
Through this the smooth deceitful waters teemed
    On dreadful wheels beneath.

They swim the river wide, nor think nor care ·—
    The waters flow,
And, by the current strong, they carried are
    Into the mill-stream now.

Through the swift waters as young Ned was rolled,
    The gulf when near,
On a kind brier by chance he laid fast hold,
    And stopped his dread career.

53

But luckless Hal was by the mill-wheel torn ;--
    A warning sad !
And the untimely death all friends now mourn,
    Of this poor truant lad.

                  ADELAIDE.

George and the Chimney-sweep

HIS petticoats now George cast off,
    For he was four years old ,
His trousers were of nankeen stuff,
    With buttons bright as gold.
' May I,' said George, ' just go abroad,
    My pretty clothes to show ?
May I, mamma ? but speak the word ;'
    The answer was, ' No, no.'

' Go, run below, George, in the court,
    But go not in the street,
Lest boys with you should make some sport,
    Or gipsies you should meet.'
Yet, though forbidden, he went out,
    That other boys might spy,
And proudly there he walked about,
    And thought—' How fine am I !'

But whilst he strutted through the street,
    With looks both vain and pert,
A sweep-boy passed, whom not to meet,
    He slipped—into the dirt.

'*The sooty lad, whose heart was kind,*
To help him quickly ran' (p. 57)

The Butterfly

The sooty lad, whose heart was kind,
  To help him quickly ran,
And grasp'd his arm, with—' Never mind,
  You're up, my little man.'

Sweep wiped his clothes with labour vain,
  And begged him not to cry ;
And when he'd blackened every stain,
  Said, ' Little sir, good-bye.'
Poor George, almost as dark as sweep,
  And smeared in dress and face,
Bemoans with sobs, both loud and deep,
  His well-deserved disgrace.

ADELAIDE.

The Butterfly

THE Butterfly, an idle thing,
    Nor honey makes, nor yet can sing,
  As do the bee and bird ;
Nor does it, like the prudent ant,
Lay up the grain for times of want,
  A wise and cautious hoard.

My youth is but a summer's day :
Then like the bee and ant I'll lay
  A store of learning by ;
And though from flower to flower I rove,
My stock of wisdom I'll improve,
  Nor be a butterfly.

ADELAIDE.

Original Poems

The Redbreast's Petition

THE thrush sings nobly on the tree,
  In strength of voice excelling me,
    Whilst leaves and fruits are on ;
But think how Robin sings for you,
When nature's beauties bid adieu,
    And leaves and fruits are gone.
Ah, then, to me some crumbs of bread pray fling,
And through the year my grateful thanks I'll sing.

When winter's winds blow loud and rude,
And birds retire in sullen mood,
    And snows make white the ground,
My note your drooping heart may charm ;
And, sure that you'll not do me harm,
    I hop your window round.
Ah, then, to me some crumbs of bread pray fling !
And through the year my grateful thanks I'll sing.

Since, friends, in you I put my trust,
And please you too, you should be just,
    And for your music pay !
Or if I find a traveller dead,
My bill with leaves his corpse shall spread,
    And sing his passing lay.
Ah, then, to me some crumbs of bread pray fling !
And through the year my grateful thanks I'll sing.

ADELAIDE.

The Nightingale

THY plaintive notes, sweet Philomel,
   All other melodies excel;
   Deep in the grove retired,
Thou seem'st thyself and song to hide,
Nor dost thou boast, or plume with pride,
   Nor wish to be admired.

So, if endued with power and grace,
And with that power my will keep pace,
   I'll act a generous part;
And banish ostentatious show!
Nor let my liberal action know
   A witness but my heart.

ADELAIDE.

Original Poems

The Lark

FROM his humble grassy bed,
  See the warbling lark arise !
By his grateful wishes led,
  Through those regions of the skies.

Songs of thanks and praise he pours,
  Harmonizing airy space,
Sings and mounts, and higher soars,
  Towards the throne of heavenly grace.

Small his gifts compared with mine,
  Poor my thanks with his compared ·
I've a soul almost divine ;
  Angels' blessings with me shared.

Wake, my soul, to praise aspire,
  Reason, every sense accord,
Join in pure, seraphic fire,
  Love, and thank, and praise the Lord.

ADELAIDE.

Washing and Dressing

AH! why will my dear little girl be so cross,
 And cry, and look sulky, and pout?
To lose her sweet smile is a terrible loss,
 I can't even kiss her without.

You say you don't like to be washed and be drest,
 But would you not wish to be clean?
Come, drive that long sob from your dear little breast,
 This face is not fit to be seen.

If the water is cold, and the brush hurts your head,
 And the soap has got into your eye,
Will the water grow warmer for all that you've said?
 And what good will it do you to cry?

It is not to tease you and hurt you, my sweet,
 But only for kindness and care,
That I wash you, and dress you, and make you look neat,
 And comb out your tanglesome hair.

I don't mind the trouble, if you would not cry,
 But pay me for all with a kiss;
That's right—take the towel and wipe your wet eye,
 I thought you'd be good after this.

A. T.

The Plum-Cake

'OH! I've got a plum-cake, and a fine feast I'll make,
  So nice to have all to myself!
I can eat every day while the rest are at play,
  And then put it by on the shelf.'

Thus said little John, and how soon it was gone!
  For with zeal to his cake he applied,
While fingers and thumbs, for the sweatmeats and plums,
  Were hunting and digging beside.

But, woeful to tell, a misfortune befell,
  That shortly his folly revealed,
After eating his fill, he was taken so ill,
  That the cause could not now be concealed.

As he grew worse and worse, the doctor and nurse,
  To cure his disorder were sent ;
And rightly you'll think, he had physic to drink,
  Which made him sincerely repent.

And while on the bed he rolled his hot head,
  Impatient with sickness and pain,
He could not but take this reproof from his cake,
  ' Do not be such a glutton again.'

A. T.

"'I can eat every day while the rest are at play.'"

Another Plum-Cake

'OH! I've got a plum-cake, and a feast let us
      make ;
Come, schoolfellows, come at my call :
I assure you 'tis nice, and we'll each have a slice,
  Here's more than enough for us all.'

Thus said little Jack, as he gave it a smack,
  And sharpened his knife to begin ;
Nor was there one found, upon the playground,
  So cross that he would not come in.

With masterly strength he cut through it at length,
  And gave to each playmate a share :
Charles, William, and James, and many more names,
  Partook his benevolent care.

And when it was done, and they'd finished their fun,
  To marbles or hoop they went back ,
And each little boy felt it always a joy,
  To do a good turn for good Jack.

In his task and his book, his best pleasures he took,
  And as he thus wisely began,
Since he's been a man grown, he has constantly shown,
  That a good boy will make a good man

                                        A. T.

For a Naughty Little Girl

MY sweet little girl should be cheerful and mild,
    She must not be fretful and cry !
Oh, why is this passion ? remember, my child,
    GOD sees you who lives in the sky.

That dear little face, that I like so to kiss,
    How alter'd and sad it appears !
Do you think I can love you so naughty as this,
    Or kiss you, all wetted with tears ?

Remember, though GOD is in heaven, my love,
    He sees you within and without,
And always looks down, from His glory above,
    To notice what you are about.

If I am not with you, or if it be dark,
    And nobody is in the way,
His eye is as able your doings to mark,
    In the night as it is in the day.

Then dry up your tears and look smiling again,
    And never do things that are wrong ;
For I'm sure you must feel it a terrible pain,
    To be naughty and crying so long.

We'll pray, then, that GOD may your passion forgive,
    And teach you from evil to fly ,
And then you'll be happy as long as you live,
    And happy whenever you die

                A. T.

Honest Old Tray

DO not hurt the poor fellow, your honest old
Tray!
What good will it do you to drive him away,
Or tease him, and force him to bite?
Remember how faithful he is to his charge.
And barks at the rogues when we set him at
large,
And guards us by day and by night.

Though you, by-and-by, will grow up to a man,
And Tray'll be a dog, let him grow as he can,
Remember, my good little lad,
A dog that is honest, and faithful, and mild,
Is not only better than is a bad child,
But better than *men* that are bad.

If you are a boy, and Tray is but a beast,
I think it should teach you one lesson at least,
You ought to act better than he;
And if without reason, or judgment, or sense,
Tray does as we bid him, and gives no offence,
How diligent Richard should be!

If I do but just whistle, as often you've seen,
He seems to say, ' Master, what is it you mean?
My courage and duty are tried '
And see, when I throw my stick over the pale,
He fetches it back, and comes wagging his tail,
And lays it down close to my side.

Then honest old Tray, let him sleep at his ease,
While you from him learn to endeavour to please,
  And obey me with spirit and joy .
Or else we shall find (what would grieve me to say)
That Richard's no better than honest old Tray,
  And a brute has more sense than a boy.

A. T.

To a Little Girl that has told a Lie

AND has my darling told a lie ?
    Did she forget that GOD was by ?
That GOD, who saw the thing she did,
From whom no action can be hid ,
Did she forget that GOD could see
And hear, wherever she might be ?

He made your eyes, and can discern
Whichever way you think to turn ;
He made your ears, and He can hear
When you think nobody is near ,
In every place, by night or day,
He watches all you do and say.

Oh, how I wish you would but try
To act, as shall not need a lie ;
And when you wish a thing to do,
That has been once forbidden you,
Remember that, nor ever dare
To disobey—for GOD is there.

€3

"And has my darling told a lie ?"

To a Little Girl that told a Lie

Why should you fear the truth to tell?
Does falsehood ever do so well?
Can you be satisfied to know,
There's something wrong to hide below?
No! let your fault be what it may,
To own it is the happy way.

So long as you your crime conceal,
You cannot light and gladsome feel:
Your little heart will seem opprest,
As if a weight were on your breast;
And e'en your mother's eye to meet,
Will tinge your face with shame and heat

Yes, GOD has made your duty clear,
By every blush, by every fear;
And conscience, like an angel kind,
Keeps watch to bring it to your mind:
Its friendly warnings ever heed,
And neither tell a lie—nor need.

A. T.

The Two Gardens

WHEN Harry and Dick had been striving to please,
  Their father (to whom it was known)
Made two little gardens, and stocked them with trees,
  And gave one to each for his own.

Harry thanked his papa, and with rake, hoe, and spade,
  Directly began his employ:
And soon such a neat little garden was made,
  That he panted with labour and joy.

There was always some bed or some border to mend,
  Or something to tie or to stick;
And Harry rose early his garden to tend,
  While sleeping lay indolent Dick.

The tulip, the rose, and the lily so white,
  United their beautiful bloom;
And often the honey-bee stooped from his flight
  To sip the delicious perfume.

A neat row of peas in full blossom was seen,
  French beans were beginning to shoot;
And his gooseberries and currants, though yet they were
    green,
  Foretold for him plenty of fruit.

But Richard loved better in bed to repose,
  And there, as he curled himself round,
Forgot that no tulip, nor lily, nor rose,
  Nor fruit in his garden was found.

Rank weeds and tall nettles disfigured his beds,
  Nor cabbage nor lettuce was seen;
The slug and the snail showed their mischievous heads,
  And ate every leaf that was green.

The Two Gardens.

My Mother

Thus Richard the Idle, who shrank from the cold,
  Beheld his trees naked and bare :
While Harry the Active was charmed to behold
  The fruit of his patience and care.

A. T.

My Mother

WHO fed me from her gentle breast,
    And hushed me in her arms to rest,
And on my cheek sweet kisses prest ?
          My Mother.

When sleep forsook my open eye,
Who was it sung sweet hushaby,
And rocked me that I should not cry ?
          My Mother.

Who sat and watched my infant head,
When sleeping on my cradle bed ?
And tears of sweet affection shed ?
          My Mother.

When pain and sickness made me cry,
Who gazed upon my heavy eye,
And wept for fear that I should die ?
          My Mother.

Who dressed my doll in clothes so gay,
And taught me pretty how to play,
And minded all I had to say ?
          My Mother.

Original Poems

Who ran to help me when I fell,
And would some pretty story tell,
Or kiss the place to make it well?
               My Mother.

Who taught my infant lips to pray,
And love GOD's holy book and day,
And walk in wisdom's pleasant way?
               My Mother.

And can I ever cease to be
Affectionate and kind to thee,
Who was so very kind to me,
               My Mother?

Ah! no, the thought I cannot bear,
And if GOD please my life to spare,
I hope I shall reward thy care,
               My Mother.

When thou art feeble, old, and grey,
My healthy arm shall be thy stay,
And I will soothe thy pains away,
               My Mother.

And when I see thee hang thy head,
'Twill be my turn to watch *thy* bed,
And tears of sweet affection shed,
               My Mother.*

                        A. T.

* See note on p 403 —ED.

The Palace and Cottage

H IGH on a mountain's haughty steep
Lord Hubert's palace stood ;
Before it rolled a river deep,
Behind it waved a wood.

Low in an unfrequented vale,
A peasant built his cell ;
Sweet flowers perfumed the cooling gale,
And graced his garden well.

Loud riot through Lord Hubert's hall
In noisy clamour ran ·
He scarcely closed his eyes at all,
Till breaking day began.

In scenes of quiet and repose
Young William's life was spent .
With morning's early beam he rose,
And forth to labour went.

On sauces rich and viands fine
Lord Hubert daily fed ,
His goblet filled with sparkling wine,
His board with dainties spread.

Warm from the sickle or the plough,
His heart as light as air,
His garden-ground and dappled cow
Supplied young William's fare.

On beds of down, beset with gold,
With satin curtains drawn,
His feverish limbs Lord Hubert rolled
From midnight's gloom to morn.

77

Original Poems

Stretched on a hard and flocky bed,
    The cheerful rustic lay ·
And sweetest slumbers lulled his head,
    From eve to breaking day.

Fever and gout, and aches and pains,
    Destroyed Lord Hubert's rest ;
Disorder burnt in all his veins,
    And sickened in his breast.

A stranger to the ills of wealth,
    Behind his rugged plough,
The cheek of William glowed with health,
    And cheerful was his brow.

No gentle friend to soothe his pain,
    Sat near Lord Hubert's bed ,
His friends and servants, light and vain,
    From scenes of sorrow fled.

But William, when, with many a year,
    His dying day came on,
Had wife and child, with bosom dear,
    To lean and rest upon.

The solemn hearse, the waving plume,
    A train of mourners grim,
Carried Lord Hubert to the tomb ;
    But no one grieved for him.

No weeping eye, no gentle breast,
    Lamented his decay,
Nor round his costly coffin prest,
    To gaze upon his clay.

But when within the narrow bed,
    Old William came to lie,
When clammy sweats had chilled his head,
    And death had glazed his eye ;

'No marble pile, or costly tomb,
Is seen where William sleeps.'

Ball

Sweet tears, by fond affection dropped,
  From many an eyelid fell;
And many a lip, by anguish stopped,
  Half spoke the sad farewell.

No marble pile, or costly tomb,
  Is seen where William sleeps;
But there wild thyme and cowslips bloom,
  And there affection weeps.

                                        A T.

Ball

'MY good little fellow, don't throw your ball there,
    You'll break neighbour's windows, I know;
On the end of the house there is room, and to spare,
Go round, you can have a delightful game there,
    Without fearing for where you may throw.'

Harry thought he might safely continue his play
    With a little more care than before;
So, heedless of all that his father could say,
As soon as he saw he was out of the way
    Resolved to have fifty throws more.

Already as far as to forty he rose,
    And no mischief had happened at all;
One more, and one more, he successfully throws,
But when, as he thought, just arrived at the close,
    In popped his unfortunate ball.

'I'm sure that I thought, and I did not intend,'
    Poor Harry was going to say;
But soon came the glazier the window to mend, ~
And both the bright shillings he wanted to spend
    He had for his folly to pay.

81

H

When little folks think they know better than great,
  And what is forbidden them, do,
We must always expect to see, sooner or late,
That such wise little fools have a similar fate,
  And that one of the fifty goes through.

A. T.

The Fox and the Crow

A FABLE

THE fox and the crow,
    In prose, I well know,
Many good little girls can rehearse :
    Perhaps it will tell
    Pretty nearly as well,
If we try the same fable in verse.

In a dairy a crow,
    Having ventured to go,
Some food for her young ones to seek,
    Flew up in the trees,
    With a fine piece of cheese,
Which she joyfully held in her beak

A fox, who lived by,
    To the tree saw her fly,
And to share in the prize made a vow ,
    For having just dined,
    He for cheese felt inclined,
So he went and sat under the bough.

'*In popped his unfortunate ball*' (p. 81).

The Fox and the Crow

She was cunning, he knew,
But so was he too,
And with flattery adapted his plan,
For he knew if she'd speak,
It must fall from her beak,
So, bowing politely, began.

' 'Tis a very fine day '
(Not a word did she say).
' The wind, I believe, ma'am, is south,
A fine harvest for peas.'
He then looked at the cheese,
But the crow did not open her mouth.

Sly Reynard, not tired,
Her plumage admired,
' How charming ! how brilliant its hue !
The voice must be fine,
Of a bird so divine,
Ah, let me just hear it, pray do.

' Believe me, I long
To hear a sweet song :'
The silly crow foolishly tries ·
She scarce gave one squall,
When the cheese she let fall,
And the fox ran away with the prize.

MORAL

Ye innocent fair,
Of coxcombs beware,
To flattery never give ear ;
Try well each pretence,
And keep to plain sense,
And then you have little to fear.

LITTLE B

85

Original Poems

Beautiful Things

WHAT millions of beautiful things there must be
In this mighty world!—who could reckon
them all?
The tossing, the foaming, the wide flowing sea,
And thousands of rivers that into it fall

O there are the mountains, half covered with snow,
With tall and dark trees, like a girdle of green,
And waters that wind in the valleys below,
Or roar in the caverns, too deep to be seen.

Vast caves in the earth, full of wonderful things,
The bones of strange animals, jewels, and spars ;
Or, far up in Iceland, the hot boiling springs,
Like fountains of feathers, or showers of stars !

Here, spread the sweet meadows with thousands of
flowers ;
Far away are old woods, that for ages remain ;
Wild elephants sleep in the shade of their bowers ;
Or troops of young antelopes traverse the plain.

O yes, they are glorious, all, to behold,
And pleasant to read of, and curious to know,
And something of GOD and His wisdom we're told,
Whatever we look at—wherever we go !

A. T.

Great Things

COME tell of the planets that roll round the sky,
And tell of the wisdom that guides them on high :
Come tell of their magnitudes, motions, and phases,
And which are the swiftest in running their races :
And tell of the moons, each in regular course,
And speak of their splendour, their distance, and force.

Hear then, child of earth, this wonderful story
Of God's works, and how they show forth His glory ;
For the stars and the planets speak much of His might,
And, if we will listen, sing anthems by night.

And first, of the sun, flaming centre of all,
Many thousand times bigger than this little ball :
He turns on his axis in twenty-five days,
And sheds through the system a deluge of rays.
Now mark his dimensions, in round numbers given,
The earth's disc as one—his, a hundred and eleven.
Yet solid and dense is his substance, like ours,
Although from his vesture a flood of light pours,
His atmosphere shoots forth a torrent of flame,
An ocean still burning, yet ever the same !
Around him revolve—and perhaps there are more—
Of planets and satellites, say fifty-four :
To him they are globules, and lost in his glare :
He's a sultan, and they are the pearls in his hair.
First Mercury travels, so near the sun's beam,
As would turn our earth's metals and mountains to
steam ,
Yet he well likes his orbit, and round it he plays,
A few hours deducted, in eighty-eight days.
Then Venus, bright lamp of the evening and morn !
Lengthens twilight on earth by her dazzling horn.

87

Original Poems

How lucid her substance ! how clear are her skies !
She sparkles a diamond as onward she hies !
The third place is held by this ocean-girt Earth,
The cloud-cover'd, wind-shaken, place of our birth :
With its valleys of verdure, its corn-fields, and downs,
Its cities of uproar, its hamlets and towns,
Its volcanoes flinging forth fiery flakes,
Its snow-crested mountains, and glassy smooth lakes.
This earth, our abode, spins about on its poles ,
And all would be dizzy to see how it rolls.
The moon too her circuit keeps constant with ours,
And in heaving our ocean, exhibits her powers.
A globe less than earth, and of murky red face,
Mars, revolves further off, and holds the fourth place ;
Like earth, he has atmosphere, land too, and seas,
And there's snow at his poles when the wintry winds
    freeze.
All near the echptic, and hard to be traced,
Twenty-six little planets we then find are placed ;
Some large one, it may be, in ages gone by,
May have burst into fragments, that roll through the
    sky.
Far remote from the sun, and yet greater than all,
Moves Jupiter vast, with his cloud-banded ball,
Eighty-seven thousand miles he measures across,
And he whirls on his poles with incredible force ;
For in less than ten hours he sees night and day,
The stars of his sky, how they hurry away !
Yet his orbit employs him a nearly twelve years,
And satellites four hold the course that he steers.
Next Saturn, more distant, revolves with his ring—
Or crown, shall we call it, and he a grave king.
And beside this broad belt of silvery light,
Eight moons with pale lustre illumine his night.
Thirty years—little less, of our times are expended,
Before a course round his wide orbit is ended.

Great Things

Uranus comes next, and 'twas fancied that he
Was the last, with his moons, perhaps six,—perhaps
    three,
For his orbit employs him, so vast is its span,
All the years that are granted, at longest, to man:
But since—O the wonders that science has done!
We have found a new planet, so far from the sun,
That but for our glasses and long calculation,
We surely should not have discover'd his station.
His name we call Neptune, and distant so far,
The sun can appear little more than a star.
But what shall we say of the comet that shows
Its ominous tail that with pallid light glows?
Wisp of vapour! that stretches from orbit to orbit,
And whirls round the sun, till the sun shall absorb it.
But solid or cloudy, these comets they move all,
In orbits elliptic, or very long oval.
And millions on millions of these errant masses
Flit about in the sky, tho' unseen by our glasses.
Such then is the system in which we revolve,
But who to pass onward through space shall resolve?
Or what wing of fancy can soar to the height
Where stars keep their stations—a phalanx of light?
Nor reason, nor fancy, that field can explore;
We pause in mute wonder, and GOD we adore.

A. T.

Deep Things

COME, think of the wonderful things there must be
 Concealed in the caverns and cells of the sea :
For there must be jewels and diamonds bright,
Lost ages ago, hidden out of our sight.

And ships too entire that have foundered in storms,
Now bristle the bottom with skeleton forms ,
Deep tides murmur thro' them, and weeds as they passed
Were caught and hang clotted in wreaths on the mast.

And then the rich cargoes, wealth not to be told,
The silks and the spices, the silver and gold ;
And guns that dealt death at the warrior's command,
Are silently tombing themselves in the sand.

But unburied whiten the bones of the crew ,
Ah ! would that the widow and orphan but knew
The place where their dirge by deep billows is sighed,
The place where unheeded, unholpen, they died.

There, millions on millions of glittering shells,
The nautilus there, with its pearl-coated cells,
And the scale-covered monsters that sleep or that roam,
The lords without rival of that boundless home.

The microscope mason his toil there pursues,
Coral insect ! unseen are his beautiful hues ;
Yet in process of time, tho' so puny and frail,
O'er the might of the ocean his structures prevail :

On the surface at last a flat islet is spied,
And shingle and sand are heaped up by the tide ;
Seeds brought by the breezes take root, and erewhile
Man makes him a home on the insect-built pile!

James and the Shoulder of Mutton

The deep then,—what is it ? A wonderful hoard,
Where all precious things are in multitudes stored ;
The workshop of nature, where islands are made,
And in silence, foundations of continents laid !

A. T.

James and the Shoulder of Mutton

YOUNG Jem at noon return'd from school,
 As hungry as could be,
He cried to Sue, the servant-maid,
 ' My dinner give to me.'

Said Sue, ' it is not yet come home ;
 Besides, it is not late.'
' No matter that,' cries little Jem,
 ' I do not like to wait.'

Quick to the baker's Jemmy went,
 And ask'd, ' Is dinner done ?'
' It is,' replied the baker's man.
 ' Then home I'll with it run.'

' Nay, Sir,' replied he prudently,
 ' I tell you 'tis too hot,
And much too heavy 'tis for you.'
 ' I tell you it is not.

' Papa, mamma, are both gone out,
 And I for dinner long ;
So give it me, it is all mine,
 And, baker, hold your tongue.

Original Poems

' A shoulder 'tis of mutton nice !
    And batter-pudding too ;
I'm glad of that, it is so good ;
    How clever is our Sue !'

Now near the door young Jem was come,
    He round the corner turned,
But oh, sad fate ! unlucky chance !
    The dish his fingers burned.

Low in the kennel down fell dish,
    And down fell all the meat ·
Swift went the pudding in the stream,
    And sailed along the street.

The people laughed, and rude boys grinned
    At mutton's hapless fall ;
But though ashamed, young Jemmy cried,
    ' Better lose part than all.'

The shoulder by the knuckle seized,
    His hands both grasped it fast,
And deaf to all their gibes and cries,
    He gain'd his home at last.

' Impatience is a fault,' cries Jem,
    ' The baker told me true ,
In future I will patient be,
    And mind what says our Sue.'

ADELAIDE

' Down fell all the meat.'

False Alarms

O NE day little Mary most loudly did call,
   ' Mamma ! O mamma, pray come here,
A fall I have had, oh ! a very sad fall.'
   Mamma ran in haste and in fear.
Then Mary jumped up, and she laughed in great glee,
   And cried, ' Why, how fast you can run !
No harm has befall'n, I assure you, to me,
   My screaming was only in fun.'

Her mother was busy at work the next day,
   She heard from without a loud cry ·
' The great Dog has got me ! O help me ! O pray!
   He tears me, he bites me, I die !'
Mamma, all in terror, quick to the court flew,
   And there little Mary she found ;
Who, laughing, said, ' Madam, pray how do you do ?'
   And curtseyed quite down to the ground.

That night little Mary was some time in bed,
   When cries and loud shrieking were heard ·
' I'm on fire, O mamma ! O come up, or I'm dead !'
   Mamma she believed not a word.
' Sleep, sleep, naughty child,' she called out from below,
   ' How often have I been deceived !
You are telling a story, you very well know :
   Go to sleep, for you can't be believed.'

Yet still the child screamed : now the house filled with
     smoke :
   That fire is above, Jane declares ·
Alas ! Mary's words they soon found were no joke,
   When ev'ry one hastened up-stairs.

All burnt and all seamed is her once pretty face,
  And terribly marked are her arms,
Her features all scarred, leave a lasting disgrace,
  For giving mamma false alarms.
                         ADELAIDE.

Sophia's Fool's-Cap

SOPHIA was a little child,
  Obliging, good, and very mild,
Yet lest of dress she should be vain,
Mamma still dressed her well, but plain.
Her parents, sensible and kind,
Wished only to adorn her mind ;
No other dress, when good, had she,
But useful, neat simplicity.
Tho' seldom, yet when she was rude,
Or ever in a naughty mood,
Her punishment was this disgrace,
A large fine cap, adorned with lace,
With feathers and with ribbons too ;
The work was neat, the fashion new,
Yet, as a fool's-cap was its name,
She dreaded much to wear the same.

  A lady, fashionably gay,
Did to mamma a visit pay :
Sophia stared, then whisp'ring said,
' Why, dear mamma, look at her head !
To be so tall and wicked too,
The strangest thing I ever knew :
What naughty tricks, pray, has she done,
That they have put that fool's-cap on ?'
                         ADELAIDE.

The Snail

THE snail, how he creeps slowly over the wall,
　　He seems scarce to make any progress at all,
Almost where you leave him you find him ;
His long shining body he stretches out well,
And drags along with him his round hollow shell,
　　And leaves a bright pathway behind him.

' Look, father,' said John, ' at the lazy old snail,
He's almost an hour crawling over the pale,
　　Enough all one's patience to worry ;
Now, if I were he, I would gallop away,
Half over the world—twenty miles in a day,
　　And turn business off in a hurry.'

' Why, John,' said his father, ' that's all very well ;
For though you can never inhabit a shell,
　　But e'en must remain a young master ;
Yet these thoughts of yours may something avail :
Take a hint for yourself from your jokes on the snail,
　　And do your *own* work rather faster.'

JANE.

I

The Holidays

'AH! don't you remember, 'tis almost December,
   And soon will the holidays come ;
Oh, 'twill be so funny, I've plenty of money,
   I 'll buy me a sword and a drum.'

Thus said little Harry, unwilling to tarry,
   Impatient from school to depart ,
But we shall discover, this holiday lover
   Knew little what was in his heart.

For when on returning he gave up his learning,
   Away from his sums and his books,
Though playthings surrounded, and sweetmeats
      abounded,
   Chagrin still appeared in his looks.

Though first they delighted, his toys were now
      slighted,
   And thrown away out of his sight ;
He spent every morning in stretching and yawning,
   Yet went to bed weary at night.

He had not that treasure which really makes pleasure,
   (A secret discovered by few),
You'll take it for granted, more playthings he wanted ;
   Oh no ;—it was something to do.

We must have employment to give us enjoyment
   And pass the time cheerful away ;
And study and reading give pleasure, exceeding
   The pleasures of toys and of play.

Old Sarah

To school now returning—to study and learning
  With eagerness Harry applied;
He felt no aversion to books—or exertion,
  Nor yet for the holidays sighed.

JANE.

Old Sarah

WITH haggard eye and wrinkled face,
  Old Sarah goes with tottering pace,
From door to door to beg ,
With gipsy hat and tattered gown,
And petticoat of rusty brown,
  And many-coloured leg.

No blazing fire, no cheerful home—
She goes forlorn about to roam,
  While winds and tempests blow :
And every traveller passing by,
She follows with a doleful cry
  Of poverty and woe.

But see ! her arm no basket bears,
With laces gay, and wooden wares,
  And garters blue and red ;
To stroll about and drink her gin,
She loves far better than to spin,
  Or work to earn her bread.

Old Sarah everybody knows,
Nor is she pitied as she goes—
  A melancholy sight.
For people do not like to give
Relief to those who idle live,
  And work not when they might.

JANE.

99

Old Susan

OLD Susan, in a cottage small,
 Though low the roof, and mud the wall,
  And goods a scanty store,
Enjoys within her peaceful shed
Her wholesome crust of barley-bread,
  Nor does she covet more.

Though aches and weakness she must feel,
She daily plies her spinning-wheel,
  Within her cottage-gate.
And thus her industry and care
Suffice to find her homely fare ;
  Nor envies she the great.

A decent gown she always wears,
Though many an ancient patch it bears,
  And many a one that's new ;
No dirt is seen within her door,
Clean sand she sprinkles on the floor,
  As tidy people do.

Old Susan everybody knew,
And every one respected too
  Her industry and care ;
And when her little stock was low,
Her neighbours gladly would bestow
  Whatever they could spare.

                              JANE.

The Gleaner (p. 103).

The Gleaner

The Gleaner

BEFORE the bright sun rises over the hill,
In the corn-field poor Mary is seen,
Impatient her little blue apron to fill,
With the few scattered ears she can glean.

She never leaves off, nor runs out of her place,
To play, or to idle and chat;
Except now and then, just to wipe her hot face,
And to fan herself with her broad hat.

'Poor girl, hard at work in the heat of the sun
How tired and hot you must be;
Why don't you leave off as the others have done,
And sit with them under the tree?'

'Oh no, for my mother lies ill in her bed,
Too feeble to spin or to knit;
And my poor little brothers are crying for bread
And we hardly can give them a bit.

'Then could I be merry, or idle, and play,
While they are so hungry and ill?
Oh no, I would rather work hard all the day
My little blue apron to fill.'

JANE.

Original Poems

Snow

O COME to the window, dear brother, and see
   What a change has been made in the night ;
The snow has quite covered the broad cedar-tree,
   And the bushes are sprinkled with white.

The spring in the grove is beginning to freeze,
   The fish-pond is frozen all o'er ,
Long icicles hang in bright rows from the trees,
   And drop in odd shapes from the door.

The old mossy thatch, and the meadow so green,
   Are hid with a mantle of white ,
The snowdrop and crocus no longer are seen,
   The thick snow has covered them quite.

And see the poor birds how they fly to and fro,
   As they look for their breakfast again ;
But the food that they seek for is hid in the snow,
   And they hop about for it in vain.

Then open the window, I'll throw them some bread,
   I've some of my breakfast to spare ;
I wish they would come to my hand to be fed,
   But they're all flown away, I declare.

Nay, now, pretty birds, don't be frightened, I pray,
   You shall not be hurt, I'll engage ;
I'm not come to catch you, and force you away,
   Or fasten you up in a cage.

I wish you could know there's no cause for alarm :
   From me you have nothing to fear ;
Why, my little fingers should do you no harm,
   Although you came ever so near !

                                        JANE.

104

' " Do look at those pigs as they lie in the straw " ' (p. 107).

The Pigs

'DO look at those pigs as they lie in the straw,'
  Willy said to his father one day;
' They keep eating longer than ever I saw,
  Oh, what greedy gluttons are they !'

' I see they are feasting,' his father replied,
  ' They eat a great deal, I allow ;
But let us remember, before we deride,
  'Tis the nature, my dear, of a sow.

' But were a great boy, such as you, my dear Will,
  Like them to be eating all day,
Or be taking nice things till he made himself ill,
  What a glutton, indeed, we might say !

' If plum-cake and sugar he constantly picks,
  And sweetmeats, and comfits, and figs,
We should tell him to leave off his own greedy
    tricks,
  Before he finds fault with the pigs.'

JANE.

Finery

IN an elegant frock, trimmed with beautiful lace,
  And hair nicely curled hanging over her face,
Young Fanny went out to the house of a friend,
With a large *little* party the evening to spend.

' Ah ! how they will all be delighted, I guess,
And stare with surprise at my handsome new dress !'
Thus said the vain girl, and her little heart beat,
Impatient the happy young party to meet.

But, alas ! they were all too intent on their play,
To observe the fine clothes of this lady so gay ;
And thus all her trouble quite lost its design ;—
For they saw she was proud, but forgot she was fine.

'Twas Lucy, though only in simple white clad
(Nor trimmings, nor laces, nor jewels she had),
Whose cheerful good-nature delighted them more
Than Fanny and all the fine garments she wore.

'Tis better to have a sweet smile on one's face,
Than to wear a fine frock with an elegant lace ;
For the good-natured girl is loved best in the main,
If her dress is but decent, though ever so plain.

JANE.

'*They were all too intent on their play,*
To observe the fine clothes of this lady so gay.'

Crazy Robert

POOR Robert is crazy, his hair is turned grey,
  His beard is grown long, and hangs down
      to his breast ;
Misfortune has taken his reason away,
  His heart has no comfort, his head has no rest.

Poor man, it would please me to soften thy woes,
  To soothe thy affliction, and yield thee support ;
But see, through the village, wherever he goes,
  The cruel boys follow, and turn him to sport.

'Tis grievous to see how the pitiless mob
  Run round him and mimic his mournful complaint,
And try to provoke him, and call him ' Old Bob,'
  And hunt him about till he's ready to faint.

But ah ! wicked children, I fear they forget
  That GOD does their cruel diversion behold ;
And that, in His book dreadful curses are writ,
  For those who shall mock at the poor and the old.

Poor Robert, *thy* troubles will shortly be o'er ;
  Forgot in the grave thy misfortunes will be ;
But GOD will His anger assuredly pour
  On those wicked children who persecute thee.

JANE.

Employment

'WHO'LL come here and play with me under
       the tree ?
My sisters have left me alone .
Ah ! sweet little sparrow, come hither to me.
    And play with me while they are gone.'

'Oh no, little lady, I can't come, indeed,
    I've no time to idle away,
I've got all my dear little children to feed,
    They've not had a morsel to-day.'

'Pretty bee, do not buzz in that marigold flower,
    But come here and play with me, do ;
The sparrow won't come and stay with me an hour,
    But say, pretty bee, will not you ?'

'Oh no, little lady, for do not you see,
    Those must work who would prosper and thrive ;
If I play, they will call me a sad idle bee,
    And perhaps turn me out of the hive.'

'Stop, stop, little ant, do not run off so fast,
    Wait with me a little and play ;
I hope I shall find a companion at last,
    You are not so busy as they.'

'Oh no, little lady, I can't stay with you,
    We are not made to play but to labour ;
I always have something or other to do,
    If not for myself, for a neighbour.'

The Fighting Birds

' What, then! they all have some employment but me,
    Whilst I loiter here like a dunce :
O then, like the sparrow, the ant, and the bee,
    I'll go to my lesson at once.'

JANE.

`

The Fighting Birds

TWO little birds, in search of food,
    Flew o'er the fields and skimmed the flood.
At last a worm they spy ·
But who should take the prize they strove,
Their quarrel sounded through the grove,
    In notes both shrill and high.

Just then a hawk, whose piercing sight
Had marked his prey, and watched their fight,
    With certain aim descended,
And pouncing on their furious strife,
He stopped the discord with their life,
    And so the war was ended.

Thus when at variance brothers live,
And frequent words of anger give,
    With spite their bosoms rending,
Ere long with some, perchance, they meet,
Who take advantage of their heat,
    Their course in sorrow ending.

JANE.

Creation

COME, child, look upward to the sky,
   The sun and moon behold!
The expanse of stars that sparkle high,
   Like specks of living gold.

Come, child, and now behold the earth
   In varied beauty stand ;
The product view of six days' birth,
   How wondrous and how grand !

The fields, the meadows, and the plain,
   The little laughing hills,
The waters too, the mighty main,
   The rivers and the rills

Come then, behold them all, and say—
   How came these things to be,
That stand in view, whichever way
   I turn myself to see ?

'Twas GOD who made the earth and sea,
   To whom the angels bow ;
That GOD who made both thee and me—
   The GOD who sees us now.

The Mountains

THE miner digs the mountain's side,
   And bores his way through rock and hill,
To search for diamonds where they hide
And lie in darkness, lone and still,
Like sparks of sunlight cased in stone,
For many a thousand year unknown.

Whence came this beautiful display
Of gems that gloomy caverns stud?
The ruby, with its crimson ray,
Like drops congealed of mountain blood?
The emerald, bright and green as spring,
Or evening light, or wild bird's wing?

How wide and large the splendid store!
The amethyst of violet blue,
The flashing sapphire, blazing more
Than sunset in its richest hue,
And rare variety of gems,
Worn but in royal diadems.

The river runs through sands of gold,
Pure veins of silver thread the mine,
In each, His bounteous hand behold,
Who bade their hidden splendours shine!
He stores them in a thousand caves,
Deep in lone hills, or roaring waves.

A. T.

115

Original Poems

The Tempest

HARK! 'tis the tempest's hollow sound,
  The bursting thunder and the rain,
While dense and heavy clouds unbound,
  In torrents fall upon the plain.

See, too, the lightning's vivid flash,
  In quick succession fire the sky;
All form a universal crash
  Of elements at enmity.

The solid earth as if with fear,
  Trembles beneath the mighty war :
The waters too in mountains rear,
  Loosed from the yoke of nature's law.

Behold the bellowing herds, the heath
  Forsake with haste, for shelter fled ;
While shepherds fly, with panting breath,
  In equal speed, and greater dread.

And see, yon ancient massive oak,
  The forest's pride for ages stood;
Its sturdy stem in shivers broke,
  Its head driven downward in the flood.

Tossed by the waves, the wretched bark,
  Alternate see it sink and rise ,
Now fixed on rocks, a shattered mark
  For furious winds and billows, lies.

In vain the drowning sailors cry ,
  Their shriek is lost while thunders roar !
In vain their moans, no help is nigh,
  Nor ship, nor hospitable shore.

The Tempest.

Turnip-Tops

And does this tempest rage in vain,
   And does no Power, with potent arm,
Its fury suffer or restrain,
   From injuring hold, or guide the harm ?

Ah yes ! a Power indeed presides,
   Yes, there's a potent Being reigns ,
Above the storm th' Almighty rides ;
   And every flash 'tis He ordains.

Then calm each fear, and silent stand,
   To learn His wisdom and His care :
The bolt, unloosed from out His hand,
   Proclaims in thunder—GOD is there.

Turnip-Tops

WHILE yet the white frost sparkles over the
      ground,
And daylight just peeps from the misty blue sky,
In yonder green fields with my basket I'm found ;
   Come, buy my sweet turnip tops—turnip-tops buy.

Sadly cold are my fingers, all drenched with the dew,
   For the sun has scarce risen the meadows to dry ;
And my feet have got wet with a hole in my shoe;
   Come haste, then, and buy my sweet turnip-tops,
     buy.

While you are asleep, with your bed-curtains drawn,
   On pillows of down, in your chambers so high,
I trip with the first rosy beam of the morn,
   To cull the green tops:—come, my turnip-tops buy.

Then with the few halfpence or pence I can earn.
  A loaf for my poor mammy's breakfast I'll buy,
And to-morrow again little Ann shall return,
  With turnip-tops, green, and fresh-gathered, to cry

A. T.

The Vulgar Little Lady

'BUT, mamma, now,' said Charlotte, 'pray, don't
      you believe
That I'm better than Jenny, my nurse ?
Only see my red shoes, and the lace on my sleeve ;
  Her clothes are a thousand times worse.

' I ride in my coach, and have nothing to do,
  And the country folks stare at me so ;
And nobody dares to control me but you,
  Because I'm a lady, you know.

' Then, servants are vulgar, and I am genteel ;
  So, really, 'tis out of the way,
To think that I should not be better a deal
  Than maids, and such people as they.'

' Gentility, Charlotte,' her mother replied,
  ' Belongs to no station or place ;
And nothing's so vulgar as folly and pride,
  Though dressed in red slippers and lace.

' Not all the fine things that fine ladies possess
  Should teach them the poor to despise ;
For 'tis in good manners, and not in good dress,
  That the truest gentility lies.'

A. T.

Meddlesome Matty

Meddlesome Matty

ONE ugly trick has often spoiled
    The sweetest and the best ,
Matilda, though a pleasant child,
    One ugly trick possessed,
Which, like a cloud before the skies,
Hid all her better qualities.

Sometimes she'd lift the tea-pot lid,
    To peep at what was in it ;
Or tilt the kettle, if you did
    But turn your back a minute.
In vain you told her not to touch,
Her trick of meddling grew so much.

Her grandmamma went out one day,
    And by mistake she laid
Her spectacles and snuff-box gay
    Too near the little maid ;
' Ah ! well,' thought she, ' I'll try them on,
As soon as grandmamma is gone.'

Forthwith she placed upon her nose
    The glasses large and wide;
And looking round, as I suppose,
    The snuff box too she spied :
' Oh ' what a pretty box is that ,
I'll open it,' said little Matt.

' I know that grandmamma would say,
    " Don t meddle with it, dear ,"
But then, she's far enough away,
    And no one else is near ·
Besides, what can there be amiss
In opening such a box as this ?'

Original Poems

So thumb and finger went to work
  To move the stubborn lid,
And presently a mighty jerk
  The mighty mischief did;
For all at once, ah! woful case,
The snuff came puffing in her face.

Poor eyes, and nose, and mouth, beside,
  A dismal sight presented;
In vain, as bitterly she cried,
  Her folly she repented
In vain she ran about for ease;
She could do nothing now but sneeze.

She dashed the spectacles away,
  To wipe her tingling eyes,
And as in twenty bits they lay,
  Her grandmamma she spies.
'Heyday! and what's the matter now?'
Says grandmamma with lifted brow.

Matilda, smarting with the pain,
  And tingling still, and sore,
Made many a promise to refrain
  From meddling evermore.
And 'tis a fact, as I have heard,
She ever since has kept her word.

A. T.

*'So thumb and finger went to work
To move the stubborn lid.'*

The Last Dying Speech and Confession of Poor Puss

' KIND masters and misses, whoever you be,
    Do stop for a moment and pity poor me!
While here on my death-bed I try to relate
My many misfortunes and miseries great.

' My dear mother Tabby I've often heard say
That I *have* been a very fine cat in my day;
But the sorrows in which my whole life has been
    passed,
Have spoiled all my beauty, and killed me at last.

' Poor thoughtless young thing ! if I recollect right,
I was kittened in March, on a clear frosty night;
And before I could see, or was half a week old,
I nearly had perished, the barn was so cold.

' But this chilly spring I got pretty well over,
And moused in the hay-loft, or played in the clover,
Or till I was weary, which seldom occurred,
Ran after my tail, which I took for a bird.

' But, ah ! my poor tail, and my pretty sleek ears !
The farmer's boy cut them all off with his shears;
How little I thought, when I licked them so clean,
I should be such a figure, not fit to be seen !

' Some time after this, when the places were heal'd,
As I lay in the sun, sound asleep in the field,
Miss Fanny crept slyly, and gripping me fast,
Declared she had caught the sweet creature at last.

125

Original Poems

'Ah me ! how I struggled, my freedom to gain,
But, alas ! all my kicking and struggles were vain,
For she held me so tight in her pinafore tied,
That before she got home I had like to have died.

' From this dreadful morning my sorrows arose .
Wherever I went I was followed with blows :
Some kicked me for nothing, while quietly sleeping,
Or flogged me for daring the pantry to peep in.

' And then the great dog ! I shall never forget him ;
How many a time my young master would set him,
And while I stood terrified, all of a quake,
Cry, ' Hey, cat!' and, 'Seize her, boy! give her a shake!'

' Sometimes, when so hungry, I could not forbear
Just taking a scrap that I thought they could spare,
Oh ! what have I suffered with beating and banging,
Or starved for a fortnight, or threatened with hanging.

' But kicking, and beating, and starving, and that,
I have borne with the spirit becoming a cat .
There was but one thing which I could not sustain,
So great was my sorrow, so hopeless my pain

' One morning, laid safe in a warm little bed,
That down in the stable I'd carefully spread,
Three sweet little kittens as ever you saw,
I hid, as I thought, in some trusses of straw.

' I was never so happy, I think, nor so proud,
I mewed to my kittens, and purred out aloud,
And thought with delight of the merry carousing
We'd have, when I first took them with me a-mousing.

' But how shall I tell you the sorrowful ditty ?
I'm sure it would melt even Growler to pity,
For the very next morning my darlings I found
Lying dead by the horse-pond, all mangled and drowned,

126

Last Dying Speech of Poor Puss

'Poor darlings, I dragged them along to the stable,
  And did all to warm them a mother was able ;
  But, alas ! all my licking and mewing were vain,
  And I thought I should never be happy again.

' However, time gave me a little relief,
  And mousing diverted the thoughts of my grief,
  And at last I began to be gay and content,
  Till one dreadful night, I sincerely repent.

' Miss Fanny was fond of a little canary,
  That tempted me more than mouse, pantry, or dairy ;
  So, not having eaten a morsel all day,
  I flew to the bird-cage and tore it away.

' Now tell me, my friends, was the like ever heard,
  That a cat should be killed for just catching a bird !
  And I am sure not the slightest suspicion I had,
  But that catching a mouse was exactly as bad.

' Indeed I can say, with my paw on my heart,
  I would not have acted a mischievous part :
  But, as dear mother Tabby was often repeating,
  I thought birds and mice were on purpose for eating.

' Be this as it may, when my supper was o'er,
  And but a few feathers were left on the floor,
  Came Fanny—and scolding, and fighting, and crying,
  She gave me those bruises of which I am dying.

' But I feel that my breathing grows shorter apace,
  And cold, clammy sweats trickle down from my face :
  I forgive little Fanny this bruise on my side '—
  She stopped, gave a sigh, and a struggle, and died !

A. T.

Day

THE sun rises bright in the air,
    The dews of the morning are dry,
Men and beasts to their labours repair,
    And the lark wings his way to the sky.
Now, fresh from his moss-dappled shed,
    The husbandman trudges along,
And like the lark over his head,
    Begins the new day with a song.

Just now, all around was so still,
    Not a bird drew his head from his wing;
Not an echo was heard from the hill,
    Not a waterfly dipped in the spring.
Now every thing wakes from its sleep,
    The shepherd-boy pipes to his flock,
The common is speckled with sheep,
    And cheerfully clamours the cock.

Now, winding along on the road,
    Half hid by the hedges so gay,
The slow waggon drags with its load,
    And its bells tinkle, tinkle away.
The husbandman follows his plough,
    Across the brown fallow-field's slope,
And toils in the sweat of his brow,
    Repaid by the pleasures of hope.

The city, so noisy and wide,
    Wakes up to a thousand affairs ;
While business, and pleasure, and pride
    Alike are intent upon theirs.

Day

The merchant with dignified look;
  My lord and my lady so grand;
The schoolboy, with satchel and book;
  And the poor hackney-horse to its stand.

For the dews of the morning are flown,
  And the sun rises bright in the sky;
Alike in the field and the town,
  Men and beasts to their labour apply.
Now, idle no hand must remain,
  Up, up, from the bed of repose,
For evening is coming again,
  And time must be caught as it goes.

And what is our life but a day!
  A short one that soon will be o'er!
It presently passes away,
  And will not return any more!
To-morrow may never arise,
  And yesterday's over and gone:
Then catch at to-day as it flies,
  'Tis all we can reckon upon.

A. T

Night

NO longer the beautiful day
　　Is cheerful, and pleasant and bright,
The shadows of evening grey
　　Are closed in the darkness of night.
The din of employment is o'er,
　　Not a sound, not a whisper is heard ;
The waggon-bell tinkles no more,
　　And hushed is the song of the bird.

The landscape, once blooming and fair,
　　With every gay colour inlaid ;
The landscape, indeed, is still there,
　　But all its fair colours are shade.
The sun sinking under the hill,
　　Is gone other mornings to make ;
The bustle of business is still ;
　　Only sorrow and sin are awake !

The busy hand, busy no more,
　　Is sunk from its labours to rest ,
Closed tight is each window and door,
　　Where once the gay passengers pressed.
The houses of frolic and fun
　　Are empty, and desolate all ;
The din of the coaches is done,
　　And the weary horse rests in his stall :

Just such is the season of death,
　　Which comes upon each of us fast !
The bosom can't flutter with breath,
　　When life's little day-time is past.

Night

The blood freezes cold in its vein,
　The heart sinks for ever to rest ;
Not a fancy flits over the brain,
　Nor a sigh finds its way from the breast.

The tongue stiff and silent is grown,
　The pale lips move never again,
The smile and the dimple are flown,
　And the voice both of pleasure and pain.
Clay-cold the once feverish head,
　The eye's pleasant flashing has ceased ;
And narrow and dark is the bed
　Where comes the grave-worm to his feast !

But as, from the silence and gloom,
　Another bright morning shall rise,
So, bursting awake from the tomb,
　We shall mount far away to the skies.
And those who with meekness and prayer,
　In the paths of religion have trod,
Shall worship all glorious there,
　Among the archangels of God.

A. T.

Deaf Martha

POOR Martha is old, and her hair is turned grey,
   And her hearing has left her for many a year,
Ten to one if she knows what it is that you say,
   Though she puts her poor withered hand close to her
    ear.

I've seen naughty children run after her fast,
   And cry, ' Martha, run, there's a bullock so bold ;'
And when she was frightened,—laugh at her at last,
   Because she believed the sad stories they told.

I've seen others put their mouths close to her ear,
   And make signs as if they had something to say ;
And when she said, 'Master, I'm deaf and can't hear,'
   Point at her and mock her, and scamper away.

Ah ! wicked the children poor Martha to tease,
   As if she had not enough else to endure ;
They rather should try her affliction to ease,
   And soothe a disorder that nothing can cure.

One day, when those children themselves are grown old,
   And one may be deaf, and another be lame,
Perhaps they may find that some children, as bold,
   May tease them, and mock them, and serve them the
    same.

Then, when they reflect on the days of their youth,
   A faithful account will their consciences keep,
And teach them, with shame and with sorrow, the truth,
   That ' what a man soweth, the same shall he reap '

A. T.

The Pin

'DEAR me! what signifies a pin!
    I'll leave it on the floor,
My pincushion has others in,
    Mamma has plenty more:
A miser will I never be,'
Said little heedless Emily.

So tripping on to giddy play,
    She left the pin behind,
For Betty's broom to whisk away,
    Or some one else to find;
She never gave a thought, indeed,
To what she might to-morrow need.

Next day a party was to ride,
    To see an air-balloon!
And all the company beside
    Were dressed and ready soon:
But she, poor girl, she could not stir,
For just a pin to finish her.

'Twas vainly now, with eye and hand,
    She did to search begin;
There was not one—not one, the band
    Of her pelisse to pin!
She cut her pincushion in two,
But not a pin had slidden through!

At last, as hunting on the floor,
    Over a crack she lay,
The carriage rattled to the door,
    Then rattled fast away.
Poor Emily! she was not in,
For want of just—a single pin!

133

There's hardly anything so small.
  So trifling or so mean,
That we may never want at all,
  For service unforeseen :
And those who venture wilful waste,
May woful want expect to taste.

A. T.

The Little Bird's Complaint to His Mistress

HERE in this wiry prison where I sing,
  And think of sweet green woods, and long to
    fly,
Unable once to try my useless wing,
  Or wave my feathers in the clear blue sky,

Day after day the selfsame things I see,
  The cold white ceiling, and this dreary house ;
Ah ! how unlike my healthy native tree,
  Rocked by the winds that whistled through the
    boughs.

Mild spring returning strews the ground with flcwers,
  And hangs sweet May-buds on the hedges gay,
But no kind sunshine cheers my gloomy hours,
  Nor kind companion twitters on the spray!

Oh! how I long to stretch my listless wings,
  And fly away as far as eye can see !
And from the topmost bough, where Robin sings,
  Pour my wild songs, and be as blithe as he.

'*Poor Emily! she was not in,*
For want of just—a single pin!' (p. 133)

The Little Bird's Complaint

Why was I taken from the waving nest,
  From flowery fields, wide woods, and hedges green ;
Torn from my tender mother's downy breast,
  In this sad prison-house to die unseen ?

Why must I hear, in summer evenings fine,
  A thousand happier birds in merry choirs ?
And I, poor lonely I, in grief repine,
  Caged by these wooden walls and golden wires !

Say not, the tuneful notes I daily pour
  Are songs of pleasure, from a heart at ease ;—
They are but wailings at my prison door,
  Incessant cries, to taste the open breeze !

Kind mistress, come, with gentle, pitying hand,
  Unbar that curious grate, and set me free ;
Then on the whitethorn bush I'll take my stand,
  And sing sweet songs to freedom and to thee.

A. T.

The Mistress's Reply to Her Little Bird

DEAR little bird, don't make this piteous cry,
  My heart will break to hear thee thus complain ,
Gladly, dear little bird, I'd let thee fly,
  If that were likely to relieve thy pain.

Base was the boy who climbed the tree so high,
  And took thee, bare and shivering, from thy nest ;
But no, dear little bird, it was not I,
  There's more of soft compassion in my breast.

But when I saw thee gasping wide for breath,
  Without one feather on thy callow skin,
I begged the cruel boy to spare thy death,
  Paid for thy little life, and took thee in.

Fondly I fed thee, with the tenderest care,
  And filled thy gaping beak with nicest food,
Gave thee new bread and butter from my share,
  And then with chickweed green thy dwelling strewed.

Soon downy feathers dressed thy naked wing,
  Smoothed by thy little beak with beauish care ;
And many a summer's evening wouldst thou sing,
  And hop from perch to perch with merry air.

But if I now should loose thy prison door,
  And let thee out into the world so wide,
Unused to such a wondrous place before,
  Thou'dst want some friendly shelter where to hide.

History of a Poor Little Mouse

Thy brother birds would peck thy little eyes,
    And fright the stranger from their woods away;
Fierce hawks would chase thee trembling through the
    skies,
    Or crouching pussy mark thee for her prey.

Sad, on the lonely blackthorn wouldst thou sit,
    Thy mournful song unpitied and unheard ,
And when the wintry wind and driving sleet
    Came sweeping o'er, they'd kill my pretty bird.

Then do not pine, my favourite, to be free,
    Plume up thy wings, and clear that sullen eye ;
I would not take thee from thy native tree,
    But now 'twould kill thee soon, to let thee fly

                                                A. T.

The True History of a Poor Little Mouse

A POOR little mouse had once made him a nest,
    As he fancied, the warmest, and safest, and
        best
    That a poor little mouse could enjoy ;
So snug and convenient, so out of the way,
This poor little mouse and his family lay,
    They feared neither pussy nor boy.

It was in a stove that was seldom in use,
Where shavings and papers were scattered in loose,
    That this poor little mouse made his hole :
But, alas ! master William had seen him one day,
As in a great fright he had scampered away,
    With a piece of plum-pudding he stole.

Original Poems

As soon as young William (who, cruel and bad,
No pitiful thoughts for dumb animals had)
   Descried the poor fellow's retreat,
He crept to the shavings, and set them alight,
And before the poor mouse could run off in its fright,
   It was smothered to death in the heat '

Poor mouse ' how it died I can't bear to relate,
Nor how all its little ones shared the same fate,
   And sunk, one by one, in the flame !
Suppose we should hear, as we may do, some night,
That William's own bed-curtains catching alight,
   He suffered exactly the same '

                            A. T.

The Chatterbox

FROM morning till night it was Lucy's delight
   To chatter and talk without stopping :
There was not a day but she rattled away,
   Like water for ever a-dropping.

No matter at all if the subjects were small,
   Or not worth the trouble of saying,
'Twas equal to her, she would talking prefer
   To working, or reading, or playing.

You'll think now, perhaps, that there would have been
     gaps,
   If she had not been wonderful clever ·
That her sense was so great, and so witty her pate,
   It would be forthcoming for ever ;

The Snowdrop

But that's quite absurd, for, have you not heard
  That much tongue and few brains are connected ?
That they are supposed to think least who talk most,
  And their wisdom is always suspected ?

While Lucy was young, had she bridled her tongue,
  With a little good sense and exertion,
Who knows, but she might now have been our
    delight,
  Instead of our jest and aversion ?

A. T.

The Snowdrop

I SAW a snowdrop on the bed,
  Green taper leaves among :
White as the driven snow, its head
  On the slim stalk was hung.

The wintry wind came sweeping o'er,
  A bitter tempest blew :
The snowdrop faded—never more
  To glitter with the dew.

I saw a smiling infant laid
  In its fond mother's arms ;
Around its rosy cheeks there played
  A thousand dimpling charms.

A bitter pain was sent to take
  The smiling babe away ;
How did its little bosom shake,
  As in a fit it lay !

Its beating heart was quickly stopped,
  And in the earth so cold,
I saw the little coffin dropped,
  And covered up with mould.

But Jesus Christ is full of love
  To babies when they die,
And takes their happy souls above
  To be with Him on high.

A. T.

The Yellow Leaf

I SAW a leaf come tilting down
  From a bare withered bough ;
The leaf was dead, the branch was brown,
  No fruit was left it now.

But much the rattling tempest blew,
  The naked boughs among ,
And here and there came whirling through
  A leaf that loosely hung.

The leaf, they tell me, once was green,
  Washed by the showers soft :
High on the topmost bough 'twas seen,
  And flourished up aloft.

I saw an old man totter slow,
  Wrinkled, and weak, and grey;
He'd hardly strength enough to go
  Ever so short a way.

His ear was deaf, his eye was dim,
  He leaned on crutches high ;
But while I stay'd to pity him
  I saw him gasp and die.

This poor old man was once as gay
  As rosy health could be ;
And death the youngest head will lay,
  Ere long, as low as he.

A .T.

Pompey's Complaint

STRETCHED out on a dunghill, all covered with
   snow,
   While round him blew many a pitiless blast,
His breath short and painful, his pulse beating low,
   Poor honest old Pompey lay breathing his last.

Bleak whistled the wind, and loud bellowed the storm,
   Cold pelted upon him the half frozen rain :
And amid the convulsions that shattered his form,
   Thus honest old Pompey was heard to complain :

' Full many a winter I've weather'd the blast,
   And plunged for my master through brier and bog ,
And in my old age, when my vigour is past,
   'Tis cruel, I think, to forsake his poor dog.

' I've guarded his dwelling by day and by night,
   Impatient the roost-robbing gipsy to spy :
And put the stout rogue and his party to flight
   With only the look of my terrible eye.

' On the heath and the mountain I've followed his flocks,
   And kept them secure whilst he slept in the sun ;
Defended them safe from the bloodthirsty fox,
   And asked but a bone when my labour was done

' When he worked in the corn-field, with brawny hot
      back,
   I watched by his waistcoat beneath the tall tree ;
And woe to the robber that dared to attack
   The charge that my master committed to me.

'When jogging from market with bags full of gold,
  No noon to enliven his perilous way,
No star twinkling bright through the atmosphere cold,
  I spied the pale robber and kept him at bay.

' One night, when, with cold overcome and opprest,
  He sunk by the way-side, benumbed in the snow,
I stretched my warm bosom along on his breast,
  And moaned, to let kind-hearted passengers know.

' Yes, long have I served him with courage and zeal,
  Till my shaking old bones are grown brittle and dry ;
And 'tis an unkindness I bitterly feel,
  To be turned out of doors, on a dunghill to die.

' I crawled to the kitchen with pitiful moan,
  And showed my poor ribs, that were cutting my skin,
And looked at my master, and begged for a bone,
  But he said I was dirty, and must not come in.

' But 'tis the last struggle, my sorrows are o'er ;
  'Tis death's clammy hand that is glazing my eye :
The keen gripe of hunger shall pinch me no more,
  Nor hard-hearted master be deaf to my cry.'

A. T.

The Leafy Spring

I LOVE the pleasant spring,
  When buds begin to push,
And flowers their nosegays bring
  To hang on every bush,
Till stores of May, with snowy bloom,
Fill the young hedge-rows with perfume.

Above the garden beds,
  Watched well by lady's eye,
Snowdrops with milky heads
  Peep to the soft'ning sky,
And welcome crocuses shoot up,
With gilded spike and golden cup.

Oh, I some meadows know*
  Beside our good old town,
Where millions of them grow,
  Just like a purple down!
They come,—but why, there's none can tell,
Only we love to see them, well.

On pastures wide and green,
  Upon a thousand stems,
Fit for a fairy queen
  To wear for precious gems,
Young cowslips smile at earth and sky,
With sweetest breath and golden eye.

* There is a beautiful spontaneous growth of the purple crocus every spring, in the meadows of Nottingham, the valley of the Trent

And where the banks are wet
   With drops of morning dew,
The gentle violet
   Steals out, in hood of blue,
And primroses in clusters rise,
Like pretty, pale-faced families.

I love the pleasant spring,
   Those days of warmth and light,
When every leafy thing
   Comes peeping into sight ;
It makes me feel,—I cannot tell
How brisk and happy, kind and well.

The Living Spring

I LOVE the pleasant spring,
   That, waking from their sleep,
Bids every living thing
   Forth into daylight creep ;
Those sunny days, so soft and warm
That make the little insects swarm

The fair white butterflies,
   Or those in gold and blue,—
Who makes them all so wise,
   As if the months they knew ?
Where, all the winter, have they slept,
That now they back again have crept ?

The Living Spring

And hark ! the merry songs
   That fill the pleasant air,
The birds, in cheerful throngs,
   To build their nests prepare ;
Those curious nests ! I would not spoil
In foolish sport such days of toil.

Far in dark woods away
   The lonely cuckoo hides,
With one soft word to say,
   And not a note besides ;
'Tis nice to hear the gentle bird
Keep practising its pretty word !

Now see the swarming rooks
   On the fresh field alight—
Like boys at lesson books,
   Chattering to say them right ;
What funny talking, as they go,
Young Master Rook and Mr. Crow !

And there the ploughman sings,
   Driving his polished share,
While up the skylark springs
   High in the morning air :
O yes ! I love the pleasant spring,
And so does every living thing !

The Pond

THERE was a round pond, and a pretty pond too,
    About it white daisies and violets grew,
And dark weeping willows, that stoop to the ground,
Dipped in their long branches, and shaded it round.

A party of ducks to this pond would repair,
To sport 'mid the green water-weeds that grew there :
Indeed the assembly would frequently meet,
To discuss their affairs, in this pleasant retreat.

Now, the subjects on which they were wont to converse,
I am sorry I cannot exactly rehearse ;
For though I've oft listened in hopes of discerning,
I own 'tis a matter that baffles my learning.

One day a young chicken that lived thereabout,
Stood watching to see the ducks pop in and out,
Now turning tail upward, now diving below ;
She thought, of all things, she should like to do so.

So the poor silly chick was determined to try ;
She thought 'twas as easy to swim as to fly :
Though her mother had told her she must not go near,
She foolishly thought there was nothing to fear.

' My feet, wings, and feathers, for aught I can see,
As good as the duck's are for swimming,' said she :
' Though *my* beak is pointed, and *their* beaks are round,
Is that any reason that I should be drowned ?

' Why should I not swim then, as well as a duck ?
I think I shall venture, and e'en try my luck !
For,' said she ('spite of all that her mother had taught her),
' I'm really remarkably fond of the water '

'*She splashed, and she dashed, and she turned herself round*' (p. 151)

The English Girl

So in this poor ignorant animal flew,
But soon found her dear mother's cautions were true:
She splashed, and she dashed, and she turned herself
round,
And heartily wished herself safe on the ground.

But now 'twas too late to begin to repent,
The harder she struggled the deeper she went;
And when every effort she vainly had tried,
She slowly sank down to the bottom and died !

The ducks, I perceived, began loudly to quack,
When they saw the poor fowl floating dead on its back ;
And by their grave gestures and looks in discoursing,
Obedience to parents were plainly enforcing.

JANE.

The English Girl

SPORTING on the village green,
The pretty English girl is seen ;
Or beside her cottage neat,
Knitting on the garden seat.

Now within her humble door,
Sweeping clean the kitchen floor,
While upon the wall so white
Hang her coppers, polished bright.

Mary never idle sits,
She either sews, or spins, or knits ;
Hard she labours all the week,
With sparkling eye and rosy cheek.

And on Sunday Mary goes,
Neatly dressed in decent clothes,
Says her prayers (a constant rule),
And hastens to the Sunday School

Oh, how good should we be found,
Who live on England's happy ground !
Where rich and poor and wretched may
All learn to walk in wisdom's way.

JANE.

The Scotch Laddie

COLD blows the north wind o'er the mountain so
bare,
Poor Sawney, benighted, is travelling there ;
His plaid cloak around him he carefully binds,
And holds on his bonnet that's blown by the winds.

Long time has he wandered his desolate way,
That wound him along by the banks of the Tay ;
Now o'er this cold mountain poor Sawney must roam,
Before he arrives at his dear little home.

Barefooted he follows the path he must go,
The print of his footsteps he leaves in the snow ;
And while the white sleet patters cold on his face,
He thinks of his home, and he quickens his pace.

But see ! from afar he discovers a light,
That cheerfully gleams on the darkness of night,
And oh, what delights in his bosom arise !
He knows 'tis his dear little home that he spies.

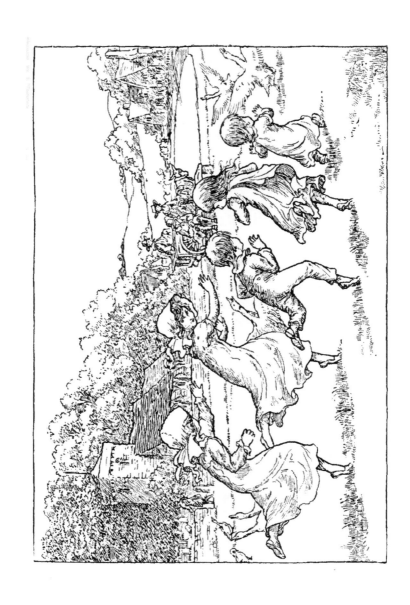

The Welsh Lad

And now, when arrived at his father's own door,
His fears, his fatigues, and his dangers are o'er;
His brothers and sisters press round with delight,
And welcome him in from the storms of the night.

For though the bleak winds of the winter may blow,
Till valleys and mountains are covered with snow;
The storms of the north cannot chill or control
The affection that glows in the Highlander's soul.

JANE.

The Welsh Lad

OVER the mountain, and over the rock,
        Wanders young Taffy to follow his flock;
While far above him he sees the wild goats
Gallop about in their shaggy warm coats

Often they travel in frolicsome crowds
Up to the top that is lost in the clouds;
Then, as they spring to the valley again,
Scale the black rocks that hang over the main.

Now when the day and his labours are o'er,
Taffy sits down at his own cottage-door;
While all his brothers and sisters around,
Sit in a circle upon the bare ground.

Then their good father, with spectacled nose,
Reads the Bible aloud ere he takes his repose;
While the pale moon rises over the hill,
And the birds are asleep, and all nature is still.

Now with his harp old Llewellen is seen,
And joins the gay party that sits on the green;
He leans in the door-way, and plays them a tune,
And the children all dance by the light of the moon

Original Poems

How often the rich, in a city so gay,
Where pleasure and luxury follow their way,
When health quite forsakes them, and cheerfulness fails,
Might envy a lad on the mountains of Wales!

JANE.

The Irish Boy

YOUNG Paddy is merry and happy, but poor,
His cabin is built in the midst of a moor;
No pretty green meadows about it are found,
But bogs in the middle, and mountains around.

This wild Irish lad is content with his store,
Enjoys his potatoes, nor wishes for more,
As he merrily sits, with no care on his mind,
At the door of his cabin, and sings to the wind.

Close down at his feet lies his shaggy old dog,
Who has plunged with his master through many a bog:
If Paddy's wild song is concluded too soon,
Shag barks a loud chorus to finish the tune.

Poor Paddy, though rude, is still grateful and kind,
But error and ignorance darken his mind.
May the voice of religion and knowledge soon sound
Within the low cabin where Paddy is found!

Then let us not laugh at his bulls and his brogue,
Nor, because he's an Irishman, call him a rogue;
But rather with kindness and charity try
His mind to instruct, and his wants to supply.

And thus, while I sing of the wild Irish lad,
The Welsh boy, and Scot, with his bonnet of plaid,
I think I shall never be tempted to roam
From England dear England, my own native home!

JANE.

Greedy Richard

'I THINK I want some pies this morning,'
  Said Dick, stretching himself and yawning ;
So down he threw his slate and books,
And sauntered to the pastry-cook's.

And there he cast his greedy eyes
Round on the jellies and the pies,
So to select, with anxious care,
The very nicest that was there.

At last the point was thus decided ·
As his opinion was divided
'Twixt pie and jelly, being loth
Either to leave, he took them both.

Now Richard never could be pleased
To stop when hunger was appeased,
But would go on to eat still more
When he had had an ample store.

' No, not another now,' said Dick ;
' Dear me, I feel extremely sick .
I cannot even eat this bit ;
I wish I had not tasted it.'

Then slowly rising from his seat,
He threw his cheesecake in the street,
And left the tempting pastry-cook's
With very discontented looks.

Just then a man with wooden leg
Met Dick, and held his hat to beg ;
And while he told his mournful case,
Looked at him with imploring face.

Dick, wishing to relieve his pain,
His pockets searched, but searched in vain ;
And so at last he did declare,
He had not left a farthing there.

The beggar turned with face of grief,
And look of patient unbelief,
While Richard now his folly blamed,
And felt both sorry and ashamed.

' I wish,' said he (but wishing's vain),
' I had my money back again,
And had not spent my last, to pay
For what I only threw away.

' Another time I'll take advice
And not buy things because they're nice ;
But rather save my little store,
To give to those who want it more.'

J<small>ANE</small>.

' " I cannot even eat this bit,
I wish I had not tasted it " ' (p. 157).

Dirty Jim

Dirty Jim

THERE was one little Jim,
    'Tis reported of him,
      And must be to his lasting disgrace,
That he never was seen
With hands at all clean,
      Nor yet ever clean was his face.

His friends were much hurt
To see so much dirt,
      And often they made him quite clean ;
But all was in vain,
He got dirty again,
      And not at all fit to be seen.

It gave him no pain
To hear them complain,
      Nor his own dirty clothes to survey :
His indolent mind
No pleasure could find
      In tidy and wholesome array.

The idle and bad,
Like this little lad,
      May love dirty ways, to be sure ;
But good boys are seen
To be decent and clean,
      Although they are ever so poor.

JANE.

N

Original Poems

The Farm

BRIGHT glows the east with blushing red,
  While yet upon their homely bed
    The sleeping labourers rest;
And the pale moon and silver star
Grow paler still, and wandering far,
    Sink slowly to the west

And see behind the sloping hill,
The morning clouds grow brighter still,
    And all the shades retire;
Slowly the sun, with golden ray,
Breaks forth above the horizon grey,
    And gilds the distant spire.

And now, at Nature's cheerful voice,
The hills, and vales, and woods rejoice,
    The lark ascends the skies;
And soon the cock's shrill notes alarm
The sleeping people at the farm,
    And bid them all arise.

Then at the dairy's cool retreat,
The busy maids and mistress meet,
    The early hour to seize.
Some tend with skilful hand the churns,
Where the thick cream to butter turns,
    And some the curdling cheese.

And now comes Thomas from the house,
With well-known cry to call the cows,
    Still resting on the plain;
They, quickly rising, one and all,
Obedient to the daily call,
    Wind slowly through the lane.

'They, quickly rising, one and all,
Wind slowly through the lane.'

The Farm

And see the rosy milkmaid now,
Seated beside the horned cow,
  With milking stool and pail ;
The patient cow, with dappled hide,
Stands still, unless to lash her side
  With her convenient tail.

And then the poultry (Mary's charge)
Must all be fed and let at large,
  To roam about again :
Wide open springs the great barn-door,
And out the hungry creatures pour,
  To pick the scattered grain.

The sun-burnt labourer hastens now,
To plod behind the heavy plough,
  And guide with skilful arm :
Thus all is industry around,
No idle hand is ever found
  Within the busy farm.

JANE.

Reading

' AND so you do not like to spell,
Mary, my dear ; oh, very well:
'Tis dull and troublesome, you say,
And you would rather be at play.

' Then I shall go at once, and look
For Mary's pretty story-book,
The poems, and the hymns to say ;
Yes, I must take them all away.

' Nay, do not fret, 'twere strange indeed
To like your books, and not to read !
And if you do not wish to spell,
To have no books will be as well.'

Poor Mary sighed with grief and shame,
And soon a tear of sorrow came !
She promised now, with humble looks,
To learn to read her pretty books.

JANE.

Idleness

SOME people complain they have nothing to do,
   And time passes slowly away;
They saunter about with no object in view,
   And long for the end of the day.

In vain are the trifles and toys they desire,
   For nothing they truly enjoy;
Of trifles, and toys, and amusements they tire,
   For want of some useful employ.

When people have no need to work for their bread,
   And indolent always have been,
Perhaps it may never come into their head,
   That wasting their time is a sin.

But time is a talent which none may abuse,
   Whatever their station may be,
The more they command it, the less they should lose,
   Nor ever make leisure a plea.

With active and useful employments combined,
   Man ever is happy and blest:
'Tis health to his body, and strength to his mind,
   Which languish from indolent rest.

Although for transgression the ground was accursed;
   Yet gratefully man must allow,
'Twas really a blessing which doomed him at first
   To live by the sweat of his brow.

                              JANE.

Original Poems

The Horse

A FABLE

A HORSE, long used to bit and bridle,
   But always much disposed to idle,
Had often wished that he was able
To steal unnoticed from the stable.

He panted from his inmost soul
To be at nobody's control—
Go his own pace, slower or faster,
In short, do nothing—for his master.

But yet he ne'er had got at large,
If Jack, who had him in his charge,
Had not, as many have before,
Forgot to shut the stable-door.

Dobbin, with expectation swelling,
Now rose to quit his pleasant dwelling,
But first peeped out, with cautious fear,
T' examine if the coast were clear.

At length he ventured from his station.
And with extreme self-approbation,
As if delivered from a load,
He galloped to the public road.

And here he stood awhile debating,
Till he was almost tired of waiting,
Which way he'd please to bend his course,
Now there was nobody to force.

The Horse

At last, uncheck'd by bit or rein,
He sauntered down a grassy lane;
And neighed forth many a jocund song,
In triumph, as he passed along.

But when dark night began t' appear,
In vain he sought some shelter near,
And well he knew he could not bear
To sleep out in the open air.

The earth was damp, the grass felt raw,
Much colder than his master's straw;
Yet on it he was forced to stretch,
A poor, cold, melancholy wretch.

The night was dark, the country hilly,
And Dobbin felt extremely chilly;
Perhaps a feeling like remorse
Just then might sting the truant horse.

As soon as day began to dawn,
Dobbin, with long and weary yawn,
Arose from this his sleepless night,
But in low spirits and bad plight.

' If this,' thought he, ' is all I get,
A bed unwholesome, cold, and wet;
And thus forlorn about to roam,
I think I'd better be at home.'

'Twas long ere Dobbin could decide
Betwixt his wishes and his pride,
Whether to live in all this danger,
Or go back sneaking to his manger.

At last his struggling pride gave way;
The thought of savoury oats and hay
To hungry stomach, was a reason
Unanswerable at this season.

So off he set with look profound,
Right glad that he was homeward bound ;
And trotting, fast as he was able,
Soon gained once more his master's stable.

Now Dobbin, after this disaster,
Never again forsook his master,
Convinced he'd better let him mount,
Than travel on his own account.

JANE.

The Good-natured Girls

TWO good little children, named Mary and Ann,
Both happily live, as good girls always can :
And though they are not either sullen or mute,
They seldom or never are heard to dispute.

If one wants a thing that the other would like—
Well,—what do they do ? Must they quarrel and
    strike ?
No, each is so willing to give up her own,
That such disagreements are there never known

If one of them happens to have something nice,
Directly she offers her sister a slice ;
And never, like some greedy children, would try
To eat in a corner with nobody by !

When papa or mamma has a job to be done,
These good little children immediately run ,
Nor dispute whether this or the other should go,
They *would* be ashamed to behave themselves so !

170

'*Two good little children, named Mary and Ann.*'

Mischief

Whatever occurs, in their work or their play,
They are willing to yield, and give up their own way :
Then now let us try their example to mind,
And always, like them, be obliging and kind.

JANE.

Mischief

LET those who're fond of idle tricks,
   Of throwing stones, and hurling bricks
And all that sort of fun,
Now hear a tale of idle Jim,
That warning they may take by him,
   Nor do as he has done.

In harmless sport or healthful play
He did not pass his time away,
   Nor took his pleasure in it ;
For mischief was his only joy .
No book, or work, nor even toy,
   Could please him for a minute.

A neighbour's house he'd slyly pass,
And throw a stone to break the glass,
   And then enjoy the joke !
Or, if a window open stood,
He'd throw in stones, or bits of wood,
   To frighten all the folk.

If travellers passing chanced to stay,
Of idle Jim to ask the way,
   He never told them right ,
And then, quite hardened in his sin,
Rejoiced to see them taken in,
   And laughed with all his might.

173

He'd tie a string across the street,
Just to entangle people's feet,
    And make them tumble down ·
Indeed, he was disliked so much,
That no good boy would play with such
    A nuisance to the town.

At last the neighbours in despair,
This mischief would no longer bear :
    And so—to end the tale,
This lad, to cure him of his ways,
Was sent to spend some dismal days
    Within the county jail.

JANE.

The Spider

'OH, look at that great ugly spider !' said Ann ,
    And screaming, she brushed it away with her
        fan ;
' 'Tis a frightful black creature as ever can be,
I wish that it would not come crawling on me.'

' Indeed,' said her mother, ' I'll venture to say,
The poor thing will try to keep out of your way ,
For after the fright, and the fall, and the pain,
It has much more occasion than you to complain

' But why should you dread the poor insect, my dear ?
If it *hurt* you, there'd be some excuse for your fear ;
But its little black legs, as it hurried away,
Did but tickle your arm as they went, I dare say.

'He'd tie a string across the street,
Just to entangle people's feet.'

The Cow and the Ass

'For *them* to fear *us* we must grant to be just,
Who in less than a moment can tread them to dust;
But certainly *we* have no cause for alarm;
For, were they to try, they could do us no harm.

'Now look! it has got to its home; do you see
What a delicate web it has spun in the tree?
Why here, my dear Ann, is a lesson for you:
Come learn from this spider what patience can do!

'And when at your business you're tempted to play,
Recollect what you see in this insect to-day,
Or else, to your shame, it may seem to be true,
That a poor little spider is wiser than you.'

JANE.

The Cow and the Ass

BESIDE a green meadow a stream used to flow,
   So clear, one might see the white pebbles below;
To this cooling brook the warm cattle would stray,
To stand in the shade on a hot summer's day.

A cow, quite oppressed by the heat of the sun,
Came here to refresh, as she often had done,
And standing quite still, stooping over the stream,
Was musing perhaps; or perhaps she might dream.

But soon a brown ass, of respectable look,
Came trotting up also, to taste of the brook,
And to nibble a few of the daisies and grass:
'How d'ye do?' said the cow; 'How d'ye do?' said
   the ass

o

Original Poems

'Take a seat,' said the cow, gently waving her hand ;
'By no means, dear madam,' said he, 'while you stand.'
Then stooping to drink, with a complaisant bow,
'Ma'am, your health,' said the ass .—' Thank you, sir,'
    said the cow.

When a few of these compliments more had been
    passed,
They laid themselves down on the herbage at last ;
And waiting politely (as gentlemen must),
The ass held his tongue, that the cow might speak first.

Then, with a deep sigh, she directly began,
'Don't you think, Mr. Ass, we are injured by man ?
'Tis a subject which lies with a weight on my mind :
We really are greatly oppressed by mankind.

'Pray what is the reason (I see none at all)
That I always must go when Jane chooses to call ?
Whatever I'm doing ('tis certainly hard)
I'm forced to leave off, to be milked in the yard.

'I've no will of my own, but must do as they please,
And give them my milk to make butter and cheese ;
Sometimes I endeavour to kick down the pail,
Or give her a box on the ear with my tail.'

'But, Ma'am,' said the ass, ' not presuming to teach—
Oh dear, I beg pardon—pray finish your speech ,
Excuse my mistake,' said the complaisant swain,
'Go on, and I'll not interrupt you again.'

'Why, sir, I was just then about to observe,
Those hard-hearted tyrants no longer I'll serve ,
But leave them for ever to do as they please,
And look somewhere else for their butter and cheese.'

The Cow and the Ass

Ass waited a moment, his answer to scan,
And then, ' Not presuming to teach,' he began,
' Permit me to say, since my thoughts you invite,
I always saw things in a different light.

' That you afford man an important supply,
No ass in his senses would ever deny :
But then, in return, 'tis but fair to allow,
They are of *some* service to you, Mistress Cow.

' 'Tis their pleasant meadow in which you repose,
And they find you a shelter from winterly snows.
For comforts like these, we're indebted to man ;
And for him, in return, should do all that we can.'

The cow, upon this, cast her eyes on the grass,
Not pleased to be schooled in this way by an ass :
' Yet,' said she to herself, ' though he's not very bright,
I really believe that the fellow is right.'

JANE.

Original Poems

The Blind Sailor

A SAILOR, with a wooden leg,
   A little charity implores;
He holds his tattered hat to beg,
   Come, let us join our little stores:
Poor sailor! we ourselves might be
As helpless and as poor as he.

'A thousand thanks, my lady kind,
   A thousand blessings on your head;
A flash of lightning struck me blind,
   Or else I would not beg my bread.
I pray that you may never be
A poor blind wanderer, like me.

'I watched amid the stormy blast,
   While fearful thunders rent the clouds;
A flash of lightning split the mast,
   And danced among the bellowing shrouds;
That moment to the deck I fell,
A poor, unhappy spectacle.

'From that tremendous, awful night,
   I've never seen the cheerful day;
No—not a spark of glimmering light
   Has shone across my darksome way.
That light I valued not before,
Shall bless these withered eyes no more

'My little dog—a faithful friend,
   Who with me crossed the stormy main,
Doth still my weary path attend,
   And comfort me in all my pain;
He guides me from the miry bog—
My poor, half-famished, faithful dog!

*' A sailor, with a wooden leg,
A little charity implores.'*

The Worm

' With this companion at my side,
   I travel on my lonely way
And GOD Almighty will provide
   A crust to feed us day by day.
. Weep not for me, my lady kind,
   Almighty God protects the blind.'

A. T.

The Worm

NO, little worm, you need not slip
   Into your hole with such a skip ;
Drawing the gravel as you glide
Over your smooth and slimy side.
I'm not a crow, poor worm, not I,
Peeping about your holes to spy,
And carry you with me in the air,
To give my young ones each a share.
No, and I'm not a rolling stone,
Creaking along with hollow groan ;
Nor am I one of those, I'm sure,
Who care not what poor worms endure,
But trample on them as they lie,
Rather than take a step awry ;
Or keep them dangling on a hook,
Choked in a dismal pond or brook,
Till some poor fish comes swimming past,
And finishes their pain at last.
For my part I could never bear
Your tender flesh to hack and tear,
Forgetting, though you do not cry,
That you may feel as much as I,

If any giant should come and jump
On to my back and kill me plump,
Or run my heart through with a scythe,
And think it fun to see me writhe.

Oh, no, I only look about,
To see you wriggling in and out,
And drawing up your slimy rings,
Instead of feet like other things ;
So, little worm, you need not slip
Into your hole with such a skip.

A. T.

Fire

WHAT is it that shoots from the mountain so
high,
In many a beautiful spire ?
What is it that blazes and curls to the sky ?
This beautiful something is—fire.

Loud noises are heard in the caverns to groan,
Hot cinders fall thicker than snow ;
Huge stones to a wonderful distance are thrown,
For burning fire rages below.

When winter blows bleakly, and bellows the storm,
And frostily twinkle the stars ,
When bright burns the fire in the chimney so warm,
And the kettle sings shrill on the bars ;

Then, call the poor traveller, covered with snow,
And warm him with charity kind :
Fire is not so warm as the feelings that glow
In the friendly benevolent mind.

Air

By fire, rugged metals are fitted for use ;
  Iron, copper, gold, silver, and tin ,
Without its assistance we could not produce
  So much as a minikin pin.

Fire rages with fury wherever it comes ;
  If only one spark should be dropt,
Whole houses, or cities, sometimes, it consumes,
  Where its violence cannot be stopped.

And when the great morning of judgment shall rise,
  How wide will its blazes be curled !
With heat, fervent heat, it shall melt down the skies,
  And burn up this beautiful world.

A. T.

Air

WHAT is it that winds about over the world,
  Spread thin, like a covering fair ?
Into each little corner and crevice 'tis curled,
  This wonderful fluid is—air.

In summer's still evening how gently it floats,
  When not a leaf moves on the spray ;
And no sound is heard but the nightingale's notes
  And merry gnats dancing away.

The village-bells glide on its bosom serene,
  And steal in sweet cadence along ,
The shepherd's soft pipe warbles over the green,
  And the cottage girls join in the song.

But oft in the winter it bellows aloud,
  And roars in the northerly blast ;
With fury drives onward the snowy blue cloud,
  And cracks the tall, tapering mast.

Original Poems

The sea rages wildly, and mounts to the skies,
  In billows and fringes of foam !
And the sailor in vain turns his pitiful eyes
  Towards his dear, peaceable home.

When fire lies and smothers, or gnaws through the
    beam,
  Air makes it more fiercely to glow ;
And engines in vain in cold torrents may stream,
  If the wind should with violence blow.

In the forest it tears up the sturdy old oak,
  That many a tempest had known ;
The tall mountain-pine into splinters is broke,
  And over the precipice blown.

And yet, though it rages with fury so wild,
  On solid earth, water, or fire,
Without its assistance, the tenderest child
  Would struggle, and gasp, and expire.

Pure air, pressing into the curious clay,
  Gave breath to these bodies at first ,
And when in the bosom it ceases to play,
  We crumble again to our dust.

                                        A. T.

Earth

WHAT is it that's covered so richly with green,
  And gives to the forest its birth?
A thousand plants bloom on its bosom serene:—
  Whose bosom?—the bosom of earth.

Hidden deep in its bowels the emerald shines,
  The ruby and amethyst blue;
And silver and gold glitter bright in the mines
  Of Mexico rich, and Peru.

Large quarries of granite and marble are spread
  In its wonderful bosom, like bones.
Chalk, gravel, and coals; salt, sulphur, and lead,
  And thousands of beautiful stones.

Beasts, savage and tame, of all colours and forms,
  Either stalk in its deserts, or creep;
White bears sit and growl to the northerly storms,
  And shaggy goats bound from the steep.

The oak and the snowdrop, the cedar and rose,
  Alike on its surface are seen;
The tall fir of Norway, surrounded with snows,
  And the mountain-ash, scarlet and green.

Fine grass and rich mosses creep over its hills,
  Flowers breathe their perfume to the gale
Tall water-weeds dip in its murmuring rills,
  And harvests wave bright in the vale.

And when this poor body is cold and decayed,
  And this warm, throbbing heart is at rest;
My head upon thee, mother Earth, shall be laid,
  To find a long home in thy breast.

A. T.

Original Poems

Water

WHAT is it that glitters in changeable green,
Or dances in billows so bright?
Ships, skimming along on its surface, are seen.—
'Tis water—that beautiful sight!

Sea-weeds wind about in its cavities wet,
The pearl-oyster quietly sleeps;
A thousand fair shells, yellow amber, and jet;
And coral grows red in its deeps.

Whales lash the white foam in their frolicsome
wrath,
While hoarsely the winter wind roars;
And shoals of green mackerel stretch from the
north,
And wander along by our shores.

When tempests awaken its waves from their sleep,
Like giants in fury they rise;
The ships now appear to be lost in the deep,
And now, carried up to the skies.

It gushes out clear from the sides of the hill;
Among the smooth pebbles it strays;
Creeps low in the valley, or roars through the mill,
And wanders in many a maze.

The traveller that crosses the desert so wide,
Hot, weary, and stifled with dust,
Longs often to stoop at some rivulet's side,
To quench in its waters his thirst.

Tit for Tat

The stately white swan glides along on its breast,
  Nor ruffles its surface serene ;
And the duckling unfledged waddles out of its nest,
  To dabble in ditch-water green.

The clouds, blown about in the chilly blue sky,
  Vast cisterns of water contain :
Like snowy white feathers in winter they fly,
  In summer, stream gently in rain.

When sunbeams so bright on the falling drops shine,
  The arch of the rainbow comes o'er,
And glows in the heavens, a beautiful sign
  That water shall drown us no more.

                                        A. T

Tit for Tat

'TIT for tat' is a very bad word,
    As frequently people apply it ;
It means, as I've usually heard,
    They intend to revenge themselves by it :
Yet places there are where 'tis proper and pat,
And there I permit them to say 'tit for tat.'

Old Dobbin, that toils with his load,
    Or gallops with master or man,
Don't lash him so fast on the road,
    You see, he does all that he can :
How long has he served you ? do recollect that,
And treat him with kindness, tis but 'tit for tat.'

Original Poems

Poor Brindle, that lashes her tail,
    And trudges home morning and night,
Till Dolly appears with her pail,
    To milk out the fluid so white .
Don't kick the poor creature, and beat her, and that,
To be kind to poor Brindle is but ' tit for tat.'

Grey Donkey, the sturdy old ass,
    That jogs with his panniers so wide,
And wants but a mouthful of grass,
    Or perhaps a green thistle beside ;
Be merciful, master, he can't carry that :
Poor donkey, they surely forget ' tit for tat.'

There's honest old Tray in the yard,
    What courage and zeal has he shown !
'Twould be both ungrateful and hard,
    Not to throw the poor fellow a bone.
He carries your basket, and fetches your hat ;
I'm sure that to starve him is not ' tit for tat.'

Poor Puss, that runs mewing about,
    Her white bosom sweeping the ground ;
The mother abused and kicked out,
    And her innocent little ones drowned :
Remember, she catches the mischievous rat .
Then be kind to poor Pussy, 'tis but ' tit for tat.'

Whatever shows kindness to us,
    With kindness we ought to repay !
Brindle, Donkey, Tray, Dobbin, and Puss,
    And everything else in its way :
In cases like these it is proper and pat
To make use of the maxim, and say, ' Tit for tat.'

                        A. T.

Jane and Eliza

Jane and Eliza

THERE were two little girls, neither handsome nor
plain,
One's name was Eliza, the other's was Jane ·
They were both of one height, as I've heard people say,
They were both of one age, I believe, to a day.

'Twas fancied by some, who but slightly had seen them,
That scarcely a difference was there between them ;
But no one for long in this notion persisted,
So great a distinction there really existed.

Eliza knew well that she could not be pleasing,
While fretting and fuming, while sulky or teasing;
And therefore in company artfully tried—
Not to *break* her bad habits, but only to *hide*.

So, when she was out, with much labour and pain,
She contrived to look almost as pleasant as Jane ;
But then you might see, that in forcing a smile,
Her mouth was uneasy, and ached all the while.

And in spite of her care, it would sometimes befall,
That some cross event happened to ruin it all ;
And because it might chance that her share was the worst,
Her temper broke loose, and her dimples dispersed.

But Jane, who had nothing she wanted to hide,
And therefore these troublesome arts never tried,
Had none of the care and fatigue of concealing,
But her face always showed what her bosom was feeling.

At home or abroad there was peace in her smile,
A cheerful good nature that needed no guile.
And Eliza worked hard, but could never obtain
The affection that freely was given to Jane.

A. T.

Original Poems

Eliza and Jane

CHEER up, my young friends, I have better news
    now,
Eliza has driven the scowl from her brow,
For finding her labours so little could win,
She turned from without, to the evils within.

'Twas a great deal of trouble, at first, I confess,
Her temper would rise, and was hard to repress;
But being a girl of some sense and discerning,
She would not be stopped by the trouble of turning.

Ten times in a day—or perhaps in an hour—
Would passion or fretfulness struggle for power;
But deaf to the whispers of weakness or pride,
For victory ten times the harder she tried.

Sometimes she would kneel in her chamber, and pray,
That GOD in His mercy would take them away;
And He, who is pleased with a penitent's cry,
Bowed down in compassion, and helped her to try.

Now, at home or abroad, there is peace in her smile,
A cheerful good-nature that needeth no guile;
And Eliza no longer is heard to complain,
That she is not beloved like her play-fellow Jane.

A. T.

The Baby

SAFE, sleeping on its mother's breast,
  The smiling babe appears;
Now, sweetly sinking into rest,
  Now, washed in sudden tears.
Hush, hush, my little baby dear,
There's nobody to hurt you here.

Without a mother's tender care,
  The little thing must die;
Its chubby hands so soft and fair
  No service can supply;
And not a tittle can it tell
Of all the things we know so well.

The lamb sports gaily on the grass
  When scarcely born a day;
The foal beside its mother ass
  Trots frolicsome away;
And not a creature, tame or wild,
Is half so helpless as a child.

To nurse the dolly gaily drest,
  And stroke its flaxen hair,
Or ring the coral at its waist,
  With silver bells so fair,
Is all the little creature can,
That is some day to be a man.

Full many a summer's sun must glow,
  And lighten up the skies,
Before its tender limbs can grow
  To anything of size,
And all that time the mother's eye
Must every little want supply.

193

P

Then surely, when each little limb
   Shall grow to healthy size,
And youth and manhood strengthen him
   For toil and enterprise,
His mother's kindness is a debt
He never, never will forget.

A. T.

The Poor Old Man

AH ! who is it totters along,
   And leans on the top of his stick !
His wrinkles are many and long,
   And his beard is grown silver and thick.
No vigour enlivens his frame,
   No cheerfulness beams in his eye,
His limbs are enfeebled and lame,
   And he seems as if going to die.

They tell me he once was as gay
   As I, in my merriest mood ;
That briskly he carolled away,
   With spirits that nothing subdued.
That he clambered high over the rocks,
   To search where the sea-bird had been ;
And followed his venturesome flocks,
   Up and down on the mountain so green.

But now what a change there appears !
   How altered his figure and face !
Bent low with a number of years,
   How feeble and slow is his pace !
He thought a few winters ago,
   Old age was a great while to come ;
And it seems but as yesterday, now,
   That he frolicked in vigour and bloom.

The Poor Old Man

He thought it was time enough yet,
  For death and the grave to prepare,
And seemed all his life to forget
  How fast time would carry him there.
He sported in spirits and ease,
  And thought it too soon to repent,
Till, all in a hurry, he sees
  The bright opportunity spent.

Now, weak with disorder and years,
  And tottering into the dust,
Oh ! he would give rivers of tears
  To have minded religion at first.
He spends his few sorrowful days,
  In wishing his life could return ;
But, alas ! he has wasted the blaze,
  And now it no longer will burn.

A. T.

The Notorious Glutton

A DUCK who had got such a habit of stuffing,
  That all the day long she was panting and puffing,
And by every creature who did her great crop see,
Was thought to be galloping fast for a dropsy ;

One day, after eating a plentiful dinner,
With full twice as much as there should have been in her,
While up to her forehead still greedily roking,
Was greatly alarmed by the symptoms of choking.

Now there was an old fellow, much famed for discerning,
(A drake, who had taken a liking for learning,)
And high in repute with his feathery friends,
Was called Dr. Drake   for this doctor she sends.

Original Poems

In a hole of the dunghill was Dr. Drake's shop,
Where he kept a few simples for curing the crop ;
Small pebbles, and two or three different gravels,
With certain famed plants he had found in his travels.

So taking a handful of suitable things,
And brushing his topple and pluming his wings,
And putting his feathers in apple-pie order,
He went to prescribe for the lady's disorder.

' Dear sir,' said the duck, with a delicate quack,
Just turning a little way round on her back,
And leaning her head on a stone in the yard,
' My case, Dr Drake, is exceedingly hard.

' I feel so distended with wind, and opprest,
So squeamish and faint, such a load at my chest ;
And, day after day, I assure you it *is* hard,
To suffer with patience these pains in my gizzard '

' Give me leave,' said the Doctor, with medical look,
As her cold flabby paw in his fingers he took ;
' By the feel of your pulse, your complaint, I've been
       thinking,
Must surely be owing to eating and drinking.'

' Oh ! no, sir, believe me,' the lady replied
(Alarmed for her stomach, as well as her pride).
' I'm sure it arises from nothing I eat,
But I rather suspect I got wet in my feet.

' I've only been raking a bit in the gutter,
Where cook has been pouring some cold melted butter,
And a slice of green cabbage, and scraps of cold meat,
Just a trifle or two, that I thought I could eat '

The Little Cripple's Complaint

The Doctor was just to his business proceeding,
By gentle emetics, a blister, and bleeding,
When all on a sudden she rolled on her side,
Gave a terrible quack, and a struggle, and died !

Her remains were interred in a neighbouring swamp,
By her friends with a great deal of funeral pomp ;
But I've heard, this inscription her tombstone displayed,
' Here poor Mrs. Duck, the great glutton, is laid ;'
And all the young ducklings are brought by their friends,
There to learn the disgrace in which gluttony ends.

A. T.

The Little Cripple's Complaint

I 'M a helpless cripple child,
  Gentle Christians, pity me ;
Once, in rosy health I smiled,
  Blithe and gay as you can be,
And upon the village green,
First in every sport was seen.

Now, alas ! I'm weak and low,
  Cannot either work or play ;
Tottering on my crutches, slow,
  Thus I drag my weary way
Now no longer dance and sing,
Gaily, in the merry ring.

Many sleepless nights I live,
  Turning on my weary bed ;
Softest pillows cannot give
  Slumber to my aching head ;
Constant anguish makes it fly
From my heavy, wakeful eye.

Original Poems

And, when morning beams return,
    Still no comfort beams for me .
Still my limbs with fever burn,
    Painful still my crippled knee.
And another tedious day
Passes slow and sad away.

From my chamber-window high,
    Lifted to my easy chair,
I the village-green can spy,
    Once *I* used to frolic there,
March, or beat my new-bought drum ;
Happy times ! no more to come.

There I see my fellows gay,
    Sporting on the daisied turf,
And, amidst their cheerful play,
    Stopped by many a merry laugh ;
But the sight I scarce can bear,
Leaning in my easy chair.

Let not then the scoffing eye
    Laugh, my twisted leg to see ·
Gentle Christians, passing by,
    Stop awhile, and pity me,
And for you I'll breathe a prayer,
Leaning in my easy chair.

                                    A. T.

Poor Donkey's Epitaph

DOWN in the ditch poor Donkey lies,
  Who jogged with many a load ;
And till the day death closed his eyes,
  Browsed up and down this road.

No shelter had he for his head,
  Whatever winds might blow ;
A neighbouring common was his bed,
  Though dressed in sheets of snow.

In this green ditch he often strayed,
  To nip the dainty grass ;
And friendly invitations brayed
  To some more hungry ass.

Each market-day he jogged along,
  Beneath the gardener's load,
And snored out many a donkey's song
  To friends upon the road.

A tuft of grass, a thistle green,
  Or cabbage-leaf so sweet,
Were all the dainties he was seen
  For twenty years to eat.

And as for sport—the sober soul
  Was such a steady Jack,
He only now and then would roll,
  Heels upward, on his back.

But all his sport, and dainties too,
  And labours now are o'er,
Last night so bleak a tempest blew,
  He could withstand no more.

Original Poems

He felt his feeble limbs grow cold,
  His blood was freezing fast,
And presently you might behold
  Poor Donkey dead at last.

Poor Donkey ! travellers passing by,
  His cold remains will see;
And 'twould be well, if all who die,
  As useful were as he

A. T.

The Orphan

MY father and mother are dead,
  Nor friend, nor relation I know ;
And now the cold earth is their bed,
  And daisies will over them grow.

I cast my eyes into the tomb,
  The sight made me bitterly cry ;
I said, ' And is this the dark room,
  Where my father and mother must lie ?''

I cast my eyes round me again,
  In hopes some protector to see ;
Alas ! but the search was in vain,
  For none had compassion on me

I cast my eyes up to the sky,
  I groaned, though I said not a word ;
Yet God was not deaf to my cry,
  The friend of the fatherless heard.

For since I have trusted His care,
  And learned on His word to depend,
He has kept me from every snare,
  And been my best Father and Friend

JANE.

Rising in the Morning

THRICE welcome to my opening eyes,
    The morning beam, which bids me rise
To all the joys of youth ;
For Thy protection whilst I slept,
O LORD, my humble thanks accept,
    And bless my lips with truth.

Like cheerful birds, as I begin
This day, O keep my soul from sin,
    And all things shall be well.
Thou givest health, and clothes, and food,
Preserve me innocent and good,
    Till evening curfew bell.*

ADELAIDE.

* Curfew Bell was ordered by William the Norman to be rung at
eight o'clock at night, at the sound of which all fire and light were
to be extinguished. The word Curfew comes from the French
couvre-feu, cover fire.

Original Poems

Going to Bed at Night

RECEIVE my body, pretty bed ;
   Soft pillow, O receive my head,
  And thanks, my parents kind,
For comforts you for me provide ;
Your precepts still shall be my guide,
  Your love I'll keep in mind.

My hours mis-spent this day I rue,
My good things done, how very few !
  Forgive my faults, O Lord ;
This night, if in Thy grace I rest,
To-morrow may I rise refreshed,
  To keep Thy holy word.

ADELAIDE.

Frances keeps Her Promise

' MY Fanny, I have news to tell,
   Your diligence quite pleases me ;
You've worked so neatly, read so well,
  With cousin Jane you may take tea.

But pray remember this, my love,
  Although to stay you should incline,
And none but you should think to move,
  I wish you to return at nine '

With many thanks the attentive child
  Assured mamma she would obey
Whom tenderly she kissed, and smiled,
  And with the maid then went away.

Frances keeps Her Promise

Arrived, the little girl was shown
  To where she met the merry band,
And when her coming was made known,
  All greet her with a welcome bland.

They dance, they play, and sweetly sing,
  In every sport each one partakes;
And now the servants sweetmeats bring,
  With wine and jellies, fruit and cakes.

Then comes papa, who says, ' My dears,
  The magic-lantern if you'd see,
And that which on the wall appears,
  Leave off your play, and follow me '

While Frances too enjoyed the sight,
  Where moving figures all combine
To raise her wonder and delight,
  She hears, alas ! the clock strike nine.

' Miss Fanny's maid for her is come.'—
  ' Oh dear, how soon !" the children cry;
They press, but Fanny will go home,
  And bids her little friends good-bye.

' See, dear mamma, I have not stayed;'
  ' Good girl, indeed,' mamma replies,
' I knew you'd do as you had said,
  And now you'll find you've won a prize.

' So come, my love, and see the man
  Whom I desired at nine to call.'
Down stairs young Frances quickly ran,
  And found him waiting in the hall.

' Here, Miss, are pretty birds to buy,
  A parrot or macaw so gay;
A speckled dove with scarlet eye .
  A linnet or a chattering jay.

203

Original Poems

'Would you a Java sparrow love?'
  'No, no, I thank you,' said the child;
'I'll have a beauteous cooing dove,
  So harmless, innocent and mild.'

'Your choice, my Fanny, I commend,
  Few birds can with the dove compare;
But, lest it pine without a friend,
  I give you leave to choose a pair.'

ADELAIDE.

My Old Shoes

YOU'RE now too old for me to wear, poor shoes,
    And yet I will not sell you to the Jews;
Yon wandering little boy must barefoot go,
Through mud and rain, and nipping frost and snow;
And as he walks along the road or street,
The flint is sharp, and cuts his tender feet.
My shoes, though old, might save him many a pain;
And should I sell them, what might be my gain?
A sixpence, that would buy some foolish toy:
No, take these shoes, poor shivering barefoot boy.

ADELAIDE.

' " *I'll have a beauteous cooing dove.* ' ·

To George Pulling Buds

D ON'T pull that bud, it yet may grow
As fine a flower as this ;
Had this been pulled a month ago,
We should its beauties miss.
You are yourself a bud, my blooming boy,
Weigh well the consequence, ere you destroy,
Lest for a present paltry sport, you kill a future j

ADELAIDE

A New Year's Gift

A CHARMING present comes from town,
A baby-house so neat ;
With kitchen, parlour, dining-room,
And chambers all complete.

A gift to Emma and to Rose,
From grandpapa it came ;
The little Rosa smiled delight,
And Emma did the same.

They eagerly examined all :
The furniture was gay ;
And in the rooms they placed their dolls,
When dressed in fine array.

At night, their little family
Must tenderly be fed ;
And then, when dollies were undressed,
They all were put to bed.

207

Original Poems

Thus Rose and Emma passed each hour,
  Devoted to their play ;
And long were cheerful, happy, kind—
  Nor cross disputes had they,

Till Rose in baby-house would change
  The chairs which were below
' This carpet they would better suit ,
  I think I'll have it so '

' No, no, indeed,' her sister said,
  ' I'm older, Rose, than you ;
And I'm the mistress, you the maid,
  And what I bid must do.'

The quarrel grew to such a height,
  Mamma she heard the noise,
And coming in, beheld the floor
  All strewn with broken toys.

' Oh, fie, my Emma ! fie, my Rose '
  Say, what is this about ?
Remember, this is New-year's day,
  And both are going out.'

Now Betty calls the little girls
  To come up-stairs and dress ,
They still dispute, with muttered taunts,
  And anger they express.

But just prepared to leave their room,
  Persisting yet in strife,
Rose sickening fell on Betty's lap,
  As if devoid of life

Mamma appeared at Betty's call—-
  John for the doctor goes ,
And some disease of dangerous kind,
  Its symptoms soon disclose

' The floor
All strewn with broken toys.'

A Cruel Thorn

' But though I stay, my Emma, you
    May go and spend the day.'
' Oh no, mamma,' replied the child,
    ' I must with Rosa stay.

' Beside my sister's bed I'll sit,
    And watch her with such care :
No pleasure can I e'er enjoy,
    Till she my pleasure share.

' How silly now seems our dispute ;—
    Not one of us she knows !
How pale she looks, how hard she breathes !
    Alas ! my pretty Rose !'

ADELAIDE.

The Cruel Thorn

A BIT of wool sticks here upon this thorn :
    Ah, cruel thorn, to tear it from the sheep !
And yet, perhaps, with pain its fleece was worn,
    Its coat so thick, a hot and cumbrous heap.

The wool a little bird takes in his bill,
    And with it up to yonder tree he flies ;
A nest he's building there with matchless skill,
    Compact and close, that well the cold defies.

To line that nest, the wool so soft and warm,
    Preserves the eggs which hold its tender young ;
And when they're hatched, that wool will keep from
    harm
    The callow brood, until they're fledged and strong.

Original Poems

Thus birds find use for what the sheep can spare .
  In this, my dear, a wholesome moral spy,
And when the poor shall crave, thy plenty share ·
  Let thy abundance thus their wants supply.

ADELAIDE.

The Linnet's Nest

' **M** Y linnet's nest, Miss, will you buy?
    They're nearly fledged.'—' Ah ! no not I ;
I'll not encourage wicked boys
To rob a parent of its joys ;
Those tender joys, to feed its young,
And see them grow up brisk and strong ,

' With care the helpless brood to nourish,
And see them plume, and perch, and flourish ;
To hear them chirp, to hear them sing,
Teach them to try the little wing,
And view them chanting on the tree
The charming song of liberty.

' 'Twould make me grieve to see them mope
Within a cage, devoid of hope,
And all the joys that freedom owns .
The prisoner's melodies are moans.
I love their song, yet give to me
The cheerful note that sings, " I'm free." ' '

ADELAIDE.

The Italian Greyhound

LIGHTLY as the rose-leaves fall,
  By the zephyr scattered round,
Let thy feet, when thee I call,
  Patting softly touch the ground.

Happy I to think thou'rt mine!
  Gentle greyhound, come apace:
Beauty's form in every line,
  Every attitude is grace.

Speaking eyes thou hast—why shrink?
  'Neath my hand why tremble so?
Beauteous greyhound, dost thou think
  Harm from me?—Believe me, no.

Cruel dogs and savage men
  Hunt a wretched hare for miles;
Guiltless greyhound, here lie then,
  Court thy mistress for her smiles.

ADELAIDE.

Original Poems

The Use of Sight

'WHAT, Charles returned !' papa exclaimed ;
  'How short your walk has been.
But Thomas—Julia—where are they ?
  Come, tell me what you've seen.'

'So tedious, stupid, dull a walk !'
  Said Charles, ' I'll go no more ;
First stopping here, then lagging there,
  O'er this and that to pore.

' I crossed the fields near Woodland House,
  And just went up the hill ·
Then by the river-side came down,
  Near Mr. Fairplay's mill.'

Now Tom and Julia both ran in .
  ' Oh, dear papa !' said they,
'The sweetest walk we both have had ;
  Oh, what a pleasant day !

' Near Woodland House we crossed the fields,
  And by the mill we came.'
' Indeed !' exclaim'd papa, ' how's this ?
  Your brother took the same ,

' But very dull he found the walk
  What have you there ? let's see —
Come, Charles, enjoy this charming treat,
  As new to you as me.'

' First look, papa, at this small branch,
  Which on a tall oak grew,
And by its slimy berries white,
  The mistletoe we knew.

214

The Use of Sight

'A bird all green ran up a tree,
    A woodpecker we call,
Who with his strong bill wounds the bark,
    To feed on insects small.

'And many lapwings cried "peewit";
    And one among the rest
Pretended lameness, to decoy
    Us from her lowly nest

'Young starlings, martins, swallows, all
    Such lively flocks, and gay;
A heron, too, which caught a fish,
    And with it flew away.

'This bird we found, a kingfisher,
    Though dead, his plumes how bright !
Do have him stuffed, my dear papa,
    'Twill be a charming sight

'When reached the heath, how wide the space,
    The air how fresh and sweet !
We plucked these flowers and different heaths,
    The fairest we could meet.

'The distant prospect we admired,
    The mountains far and blue;
A mansion here, a cottage there .
    See, here's the sketch we drew.

'A splendid sight we next beheld,
    The glorious setting sun,
In clouds of crimson, purple, gold;
    His daily race was done.'

'True taste with knowledge,' said papa,
    'By observation's gained,
You've both used well the gift of sight,
    And thus reward obtained.

215

Original Poems

' My Julia in this desk will find
    A drawing-box quite new :
And, Thomas, now this telescope,
    I think, is quite your due.

' And toys, or still more useful gifts,
    For Charles, too, shall be bought,
When he can see the works of God,
    And prize them as he ought.'

ADELAIDE.

The Morning's Task

' SIT to your books,' the father said,
    ' Nor play nor trifle, laugh nor talk ;
And when at noon you've spelt and read,
    I'll take you all a pleasant walk.'
He left the room, the boys sat still,
    Each gravely bent upon his task,
Except the youngest, little Will,
    Who yet of this and that would ask.

' I've lost my ball,' the prattler cried,
    ' Has either of you seen my ball ?'
' Pray mind your book,' young Charles replied ;
    ' Your noisy talk disturbs us all
Remember now what we were told,
    The time, I warn you, Will, draws near.'
' And what care I ?' said Will, so bold,
    ' I shall be ready, never fear.'

'*Then through the window, with a bound.*
Will jumped' (p. 210).

The Morning's Task

He spun his top, he smacked his whip,
　At marbles also he would play,
And round the room he chose to skip,
　And thus his moments slipt away.
But at the window what comes in ?
　A dazzling painted butterfly !
' A prize ! a prize which I must win !'
　Young William loud is heard to cry.

Quick on the table up he leaps,
　Then on the chairs and sofa springs ;
Now here, now there, he softly creeps,
　And now his books and hat he flings.
The brilliant insect fluttered round,
　And out again it gaily flew !
Then through the window, with a bound,
　Will jumped, and said, ' I'll soon have you.'

From flower to flower the boy it led,
　While he pursued the pretty thing :
Away it sprang from bed to bed,
　Now sipping dew, now on the wing.
And to the fields it took its flight,
　He thought the prize was worth the chase ,
O'er hedge and ditch with all his might,
　He followed still the pleasing race

To catch it he was much perplexed,
　The insect now he sees no more ;
While standing thus confounded, vexed,
　He hears the village clock strike four.
Towards home he hastens at the sound,
　All shame, surprise, and fear, and doubt :
Nor sisters, brothers, could be found
　He asks, and hears they're all gone out.

With sorrow struck, when this was told,
  He wept, and down in sadness sat.
Now o'er the stones a carriage rolled,
  And at the door came—rat, tat, tat
Then from the coach the girls and boys
  Stepped out, all smiling, pleased, and gay,
And books, and dolls, and pretty toys,
  Bats, ninepins, hoops, and kites had they.

' Ah, William !' then the father said,
  ' Come hither, child, but wherefore cry ?
Why droop your face, why hang your head ?
  Where is the pretty butterfly ?
I kept my promise, home I came,
  According to my first intent ;
You broke your word, and yours the shame,
  And we, without you, shopping went.'

JANE

The Oak

THE oak, for grandeur, strength, and noble size,
  Excels all trees that in the forest grow ;
From acorn small that trunk, those branches rise,
  To which such signal benefits we owe.

Behold what shelter in its ample shade,
  From noon-tide sun, or from the drenching rain !
And of its timber stanch vast ships are made,
  To bear rich cargoes o'er the watery main

ADELAIDE.

Careless Matilda

' AGAIN, Matilda, is your work undone !
   Your scissors, where are they ? your thimble,
      gone ?
Your needles, pins, and thread and tapes all lost ;
Your housewife here, and there your work-bag tossed.
Fie, fie, my child ! indeed this will not do,
Your hair uncombed, your frock in tatters, too ;
I'm now resolved no more delays to grant,
To learn of her, I'll send you to your aunt.'
In vain Matilda wept, entreated, prayed,
In vain a promise of amendment made.

Arrived at Austere Hall, Matilda sighed,
By Lady Rigid when severely eyed
' You read and write, and work well, as I'm told,
Are gentle, kind, good-natured, and not bold ;
But very careless, negligent, and wild—
You'll leave me, as I hope, a different child.'

The little girl next morn a favour asks :
' I wish to take a walk.'—' Go, learn your tasks,'
Replies her aunt, ' nor fruitlessly repine .
Your room you'll leave not till you're called to dine.'
As there Matilda sat, o'erwhelmed with shame,
A dame appeared, Disorder was her name :
Her hair and dress neglected—soiled her face,
Her mien unseemly, and devoid of grace.

' Here, child,' said she, ' my mistress sends you this,
A bag of silks—a flower, not worked amiss—
A polyanthus bright, and wondrous gay,
You'll copy it by noon, she bade me say.'
Disorder grinned, and shuffling walked away.

Original Poems

Entangled were the silks of every hue,
Confused and mixed were shades of pink, green, blue;
She took a thread, compared it with the flower :
' To finish this is not within my power.
Well-sorted silks had Lady Rigid sent,
I might have worked, if such was her intent.'
She sighed, and melted into sobs and tears ·
She hears a step, and at the door appears
A pretty maiden, clean, well-dressed, and neat,
Her voice was soft, her looks sedate, yet sweet.
' My name is Order : do not cry, my love ;
Attend to me, and thus you may improve.'
She took the silks, and drew out shade by shade,
In separate skeins, and each with care she laid ;
Then smiling kindly, left the little maid.

Matilda now resumes her sweet employ,
And sees the flower complete—how great her joy !
She leaves the room—' I've done my task,' she cries ;
The lady looked, and scarce believed her eyes ,
Yet soon her harshness changed to glad surprise :
' Why, this is well, a very pretty flower,
Worked so exact, and done within the hour !
And now amuse yourself, and walk, or play.'
Thus passed Matilda this much dreaded day.
At all her tasks, Disorder would attend ;
At all her tasks, still Order stood her friend.
With tears and sighs her studies oft began,
These into smiles were changed by Order's plan.
No longer Lady Rigid seemed severe :
The negligent alone her eye need fear.

And now the day, the wished-for day is come,
When young Matilda may revisit home.
' You quit me, child, but oft to mind recall
The time you spent with me at Austere Hall.

The Mushroom Girl

And now, my dear, I'll give you one of these
To be your maid—take with you which you please
What! from Disorder do you frightened start?'
Matilda clasped sweet Order to her heart,
And said, 'From thee, best friend, I'll never part.'

JANE.

The Mushroom Girl

'TIS surely time for me to rise,
   Though yet the dawn is grey;
Sweet sleep, O quit my closing eyes,
   For I must now away:—
   Each young bird twitters on the spray.

It is not for the dewy mead
   I leave my soft repose,
Where daisies nod, and lambkins feed;
   But where the mushroom grows·
   And that my widowed mother knows.

I'll rove the wide heath far and near,
   Of mushrooms fine in quest,
But you, remain, kind mother, here,
   Lie still, and take your rest,
   Although with poverty oppressed

No toad-stool in my basket found,
   My mushrooms when I sell,
I'll buy some bread; our labours crowned,
   Then let our neighbours tell,
   That you and I live wondrous well.

ADELAIDE.

Birds, Beasts, and Fishes

THE Dog will come when he is called,
   The Cat will walk away;
The Monkey's cheek is very bald;
   The Goat is fond of play.
The Parrot is a prate-apace,
   Yet knows not what he says.
The noble Horse will win the race,
   Or draw you in a chaise.

The Pig is not a feeder nice,
   The Squirrel loves a nut,
The Wolf would eat you in a trice,
   The Buzzard's eyes are shut.
The Lark sings high up in the air,
   The Linnet in the tree;
The Swan he has a bosom fair,
   And who so proud as he?

Oh, yes, the Peacock is more proud,
   Because his tail has eyes,
The Lion roars so very loud,
   He'd fill you with surprise.
The Raven's coat is shining black,
   Or, rather, raven grey
The Camel's bunch is on his back,
   The Owl abhors the day.

The Sparrow steals the cherry ripe,
   The Elephant is wise,
The Blackbird charms you with his pipe,
   The false Hyena cries

Birds, Beasts, and Fishes

The Hen guards well her little chicks,
  The Cow—her hoof is slit .
The Beaver builds with mud and sticks,
  The Lapwing cries ' peewit.'

The little Wren is very small,
  The Humming-bird is less ;
The Lady-bird is least of all,
  And beautiful in dress.
The Pelican she loves her young,
  The Stork its parent loves ;
The Woodcock's bill is very long,
  And innocent are Doves.

The streakèd Tiger's fond of blood,
  The Pigeon feeds on peas,
The Duck will gobble in the mud,
  The Mice will eat your cheese
A Lobster's black, when boiled he's red,
  The harmless Lamb must bleed .
The Cod-fish has a clumsy head,
  The Goose on grass will feed.

The lady in her gown of silk,
  The little Worm may thank ,
The sick man drinks the Ass's milk,
  The Weasel's long and lank.
The Buck gives us a venison dish,
  When hunted for the spoil
The Shark eats up the little fish,
  The Whale produces oil.

The Glow-worm shines the darkest night,
  With lantern in its tail .
The Turtle is the cit's delight,
  And wears a coat of mail.

Original Poems

In Germany they hunt the Boar,
  The Bee brings honey home,
The Ant lays up a winter store,
  The Bear loves honey-comb.

The Eagle has a crooked beak,
  The Plaice has orange spots ;
The Starling, if he's taught, will speak ;
  The Ostrich walks and trots.
The child that does not these things know,
  Might well be called a dunce ;
But I in knowledge quick will grow,
  For youth can come but once.

ADELAIDE.

The Vine

'TWAS holiday-time, and young Harry was gay,
  Though bleak the wide landscape around ;
'Twas Christmas, and homeward he tripped it away,
  For hard was the frost-bitten ground.

He ran through the garden, the pleasure-grounds too,
  The walks and dark alleys he traced ;
Admired the tall cypress, the privet, and yew,
  And holly with red berries graced :

The laurel and bay, and such fine evergreens,
  In verdure and beauty arose ;
He stopped at a tree, and he cried out, ' What means
  This leafless old tree among those ?

' Dig it up, pull it down—not a leaf on its spray,
  No shelter is here for the birds !'
But his father replied, ' I hear what you say ;
  Next autumn remember your words.'

226

The Vine

And now, as was promised, that autumn was come,
  Young Harry left school for a week;
And ripe was the nectarine, ripe was the plum,
  And peach too, with down on its cheek.

When straight to the garden our schoolboy repaired,
  Where fruit hung all tempting and fine,
'What tree,' he exclaimed, 'can at all be compared,
  Papa, with this beautiful vine?

'What bunches! what clusters! the sight is a treat!
  So charming I never did see:
The sight is delicious; the flavour how sweet!
  Oh, father, how precious a tree!'

'This tree,' said papa, 'is the one you despised,
  Which then looked so withered and bare;
But you see, by exterior few things can be prized:
  Of hasty decisions beware.

'Remember, my child, not to judge by the eye,
  Of those who in form do not shine;
And now gain a lesson, of use by and by,
  From your folly in spurning the vine.'

ADELAIDE.

Original Poems

The Spider and his Wife

IN a dark little crack, half a yard from the ground,
　　An honest old spider resided:
So pleasant, and snug, and convenient 'twas found,
That his friends came to see it from many miles round:
　　It seemed for his pleasure provided.

Of the cares, and fatigues, and distresses of life,
　　This spider was thoroughly tired;
So, leaving those scenes of distraction and strife
(His children all settled), he came with his wife
　　To live in this cranny retired.

He thought that the little his wife would consume,
　　'Twould be easy for him to provide her;
Forgetting he lived in a gentleman's room,
Where came, every morning, a maid and a broom,
　　Those pitiless foes to a spider!

For when (as sometimes it would chance to befall)
　　The moment his web was completed,
Brush—came the great broom down the side of the wall,
And, perhaps, carried with it web, spider, and all,
　　He thought himself cruelly treated.

One day, when their cupboard was empty and dry,
　　His wife (Mrs. Hairy-leg Spinner)
Said to him, ' Dear, go to the cobweb and try
If you can't find the leg or the wing of a fly,
　　Just a bit of a relish for dinner.'

228

The Poppy

Directly he went, his long search to resume,
  (For nothing he ever denied her),
Alas ! little guessing his terrible doom ;
Just then came the gentleman into the room,
  And saw the unfortunate spider.

So while the poor insect, in search of his pelf,
  In the cobweb continued to linger,
The gentleman reached a long cane from the shelf,
(For certain good reasons, best known to himself,
  Preferring his stick to his finger .)

Then presently poking him down to the floor,
  Nor stopping at all to consider,
With one horrid crash the whole business was o'er,
The poor little spider was heard of no more,
  To the lasting distress of his widow !

                                        JANE.

The Poppy

HIGH on a bright and sunny bed
    A scarlet poppy grew,
And up it held its staring head,
    And thrust it full in view.

Yet no attention did it win,
    By all these efforts made,
And less unwelcome had it been
    In some retired shade.

Although within its scarlet breast
    No sweet perfume was found,
It seemed to think itself the best
    Of all the flowers around.

From this may I a hint obtain,
   And take great care indeed,
Lest I appear as pert and vain
   As does this gaudy weed.

JANE.

The Violet

DOWN in a green and shady bed,
   A modest violet grew,
Its stalk was bent, it hung its head.
   As if to hide from view.

And yet it was a lovely flower,
   Its colour bright and fair ,
It might have graced a rosy bower,
   Instead of hiding there.

Yet thus it was content to bloom,
   In modest tints arrayed ,
And there diffused a sweet perfume,
   Within the silent shade.

Then let me to the valley go
   This pretty flower to see ;
That I may also learn to grow
   In sweet humility.

JANE.

The Way to be Happy

HOW pleasant it is at the end of the day,
  No follies to have to repent,
But reflect on the past, and be able to say,
  My time has been properly spent!

When I've finished my business with patience and
    care,
  And been good, and obliging, and kind,
I lie on my pillow, and sleep away there,
  With a happy and peaceable mind.

Instead of all this, if it must be confest
  That I careless and idle have been,
I lie down as usual, and go to my rest,
  But feel discontented within.

Then, as I dislike all the trouble I've had,
  In future I'll try to prevent it,
For I never am naughty without being sad,
  Or good—without being contented.

JANE.

231

Original Poems

Contented John

ONE honest John Tomkins, a hedger and ditcher,
   Although he was poor, did not want to be richer:
For all such vain wishes to him were prevented
By a fortunate habit of being contented

Though cold were the weather, or dear were the food,
John never was found in a murmuring mood;
For this he was constantly heard to declare,
What he could not prevent he would cheerfully bear.

'For, why should I grumble and murmur?' he said,
'If I cannot get meat, I'll be thankful for bread;
And though fretting may make my calamities deeper,
It never can cause bread and cheese to be cheaper.'

If John was afflicted with sickness or pain,
He wished himself better, but did not complain,
Nor lie down to fret in despondence and sorrow,
But said, that he hoped to be better to-morrow.

If any one wronged him, or treated him ill,
Why, John was good-natured and sociable still;
For he said, that revenging the injury done
Would be making two rogues, where there need be but
   one.

And thus honest John, though his station was humble,
Passed through this sad world without even a grumble
And 'twere well if some folk, who are greater and richer,
Would copy John Tomkins, the hedger and ditcher

JANE.

The Gaudy Flower

WHY does my Anna toss her head,
  And look so scornfully around,
As if she scarcely deigned to tread
  Upon the daisy-dappled ground ?

Does fancied beauty fire thine eye,
  The brilliant tint, the satin skin ?
Does the loved glass, in passing by,
  Reflect a graceful form and thin ?

Alas ! that form, and brilliant fire,
  Will never win beholder's love ;
It may, indeed, make fools admire,
  But ne'er the wise and good can move.

So grows the tulip, gay and bold,
  The broadest sunshine its delight ;
Like rubies, or like burnished gold,
  It shows its petals, glossy bright.

But who the gaudy floweret crops,
  As if to court a sweet perfume !
Admired it blows, neglected drops,
  And sinks unheeded to its doom.

The virtues of the heart may move
  Affections of a genial kind ,
While beauty fails to stir our love,
  And wins the eye, but not the mind.

                                        T.

Original Poems

Negligent Mary

AH, Mary! what, do you for dolly not care?
　　And why is she left on the floor?
Forsaken, and covered with dust, I declare;
　　With you I must trust her no more

I thought you were pleased, as you took her so gladly,
　　When on your birthday she was sent;
Did I ever suppose you would use her so sadly?
　　Was that, do you think, what I meant?

With her bonnet of straw you once were delighted,
　　And trimmed it so pretty with pink;
But now it is crumpled, and dolly is slighted:
　　Her nurse quite forgets her, I think.

Suppose now—for Mary is *dolly* to me,
　　Whom I love to see tidy and fair—
Suppose I should leave you, as dolly I see,
　　In tatters, and comfortless there.

But dolly feels nothing, as you do, my dear,
　　Nor cares for her negligent nurse:
If I were as careless as you are, I fear,
　　Your lot, and my fault, would be worse.

And therefore it is, in my Mary, I strive
　　To check every fault that I see:
Mary's doll is but waxen—mamma's is alive,
　　And of far more importance than she.

　　　　　　　　　　　　　　　　T.

'*Ah, Mary! what, do you for dolly not care?*'

December Night

DARK and dismal is the night,
  Beating rain, and wind so high !
Close the window-shutters tight,
  And the cheerful fire draw nigh.

Hear the blast in dreadful chorus,
  Roaring through the naked trees,
Just like thunder bursting o'er us;
  Now they murmur, now they cease.

Think how many on the wild
  Wander in this dreadful weather :
Some poor mother with her child,
  Scarce can keep her rags together.

Or a wretched family
  'Neath some mud-walled ruined shed
Shrugging close together, lie
  On the earth—their only bed.

While we sit within so warm,
  Sheltered, comfortable, safe,
Think how many bide the storm,
  Who no home nor shelter have.

Glad, these sorrows could we lighten,
  We who suffer no such woe ,
Let, at least, contentment brighten
  Every tranquil hour we know.

                    ISAAC TAYLOR.

Poverty

I SAW an old cottage of clay,
  And only of mud was the floor;
It was all falling into decay,
  And the snow drifted in at the door.

Yet there a poor family dwelt,
  In a hovel so dismal and rude ;
And though gnawing hunger they felt,
  They had not a morsel of food.

The children were crying for bread,
  And to their poor mother they'd run ;
' Oh, give us some breakfast,' they said,
  Alas ! their poor mother had none.

She viewed them with looks of despair .
  She said (and I'm sure it was true),
' 'Tis not for myself that I care,
  But, my poor little children, for you.'

Oh then, let the wealthy and gay
  But see such a hovel as this,
That in a poor cottage of clay
  They may know what true misery is.

And what I may have to bestow
  I never will squander away,
While many poor people I know
  Around me are wretched as they.

                                    JANE.

The Village Green

ON the cheerful village green,
 Skirted round with houses small,
All the boys and girls are seen,
 Playing there with hoop and ball.

Now they frolic hand in hand,
 Making many a merry chain;
Then they form a warlike band,
 Marching o'er the level plain.

Now ascends the worsted ball,
 High it rises in the air,
Or against the cottage wall,
 Up and down it bounces there.

Then the hoop, with even pace,
 Runs before the merry throngs;
Joy is seen in every face,
 Joy is heard in cheerful songs.

Rich array, and mansions proud,
 Gilded toys, and costly fare,
Would not make the little crowd
Half so happy as they are.

Then, contented with my state,
 Where true pleasure may be seen,
Let me envy not the great,
 On a cheerful village green.

JANE.

Original Poems

Ruin and Success

PART I.—THE RACE-HORSE.

' INDEED !' said my lord to his steward, ''tis droll !
 The mare and the she-ass, you say,
This morning have each had a beautiful foal,
 Two capital gifts in one day !

' I've promised the first to my neighbour, the 'squire,
 The other bestow as you will.'
The steward, fulfilling his lordship's desire,
 Gave Jack to poor Joe near the mill.

With care and expense the fine colt was brought up,
 So elegant, sleek, and so slim .
What joy ! when he started and won a prize-cup ;
 Then no horse was equal to him.

Expense was increased he was exercised, trained ;
 At first many matches he won :
But once losing more than he ever had gained,
 His master, the 'squire, was undone.

PART II.—THE ASS.

The other present, poor Jack Ass,
 A different training had
And thus with him it came to pass,
 His lot was very bad.

No groom had he ; nor oats nor hay,
 Were offered to his taste ;
And hot or cold, through night and day,
 He wandered on the waste.

Ruin and Success

His master's sons, three ragged boys,
  At once upon him rode;
And as they had no other toys,
  They teased him with a goad.

Although his usage was unkind,
  He never did them wrong;
He ate his thistles, never pined,
  And grew up stout and strong.

Poor Joe cut faggots in the wood,
  And carried them to sell;
But for the ass to bear the load,
  He thought might be as well.

To dig his garden he would stay,
  And send to town his son;
Thus gained more money every day
  Than he before had done.

His garden now had beans and peas,
  Potatoes sweet and big:
He bought a hen, and ducks and geese ·
  At length he bought a pig.

And off the waste, with money earned,
  He bought a piece of land.
And this same Joe—a farmer turned—
  Had always cash in hand.

Yet not unmindful of poor Jack,
  That helped him so to rise,
Provides him now a plenteous rack,
  And stable, where he lies.

'Thou art,' says he, 'poor beast, grown old,
  Thy toilsome days are o'er;
No hunger shalt thou feel, nor cold,
  And thou shalt work no more.

Original Poems

‘ With grateful care I grant to thee
  This comfortable shed :
When I had none, thou gain'dst for me
  My hard-earned daily bread.’

ADELAIDE

Dew and Hail

YOUNG Tommy most things well discerned :
    He read and understood,
  His memory was good ;
He taught his little sister what he learned.

Said he, ‘ ’Tis morn, but by and by,
  Those dews that wet our feet,
  The sun will by its heat
Draw up in clouds, to hang around the sky.

‘ At eve, when he withdraws his powers,
  Those dews then gently fall,
  At night refreshing all,
The tender grass, the plants, and blooming flowers.

‘ Those small white stones, that kill the grub and snail,
Are frozen water-drops, these we call hail
The large ones, that descend in mighty force,
A vast way come, and gather in their course ;
Passing through regions cold, of ice and snow,
They still congeal, and large and larger grow :
So large, that one has weighed near half a pound :
Some are like stars, some oblong, most are round,
Some hang on trees, like icicles or spars :
Those come with thunder that are shaped like stars,

Crust and Crumb

Some have killed birds, broke windows, slates, and tiles,
And scattered devastation round for miles.
The LORD, though merciful, is yet severe;
And while we love Him let us also fear.'

ADELAIDE.

Crust and Crumb

I CAN'T eat all my bread indeed;
   Mamma yet says I must:
This piece of crumb I do not need;
   I've eaten all the crust.

We never should throw bread away,
   It is a sin to waste;
Yon poor boy's glances seem to say,
   'I wish I had a taste.'

Step hither, and you shall have some,
   Come here, my little man;
You think there's crust, 'tis only crumb,
   But eat it if you can.

He eats with such delightful glee,
   His eyes are brimmed with joy;
How very hungry he must be,
   Unhappy little boy!

The day of hunger and distress
   As yet I never knew;
And for the plenty I possess,
   O LORD! my thanks are due.

And now I feel another's grief,
   And now myself I know;
Whene'er my heart would give relief,
   My hand shall not be slow.

ADELAIDE,

Original Poems

The Truant

AH! why did I, unthinking youth,
　　From school a truant stay?
To parents why not tell the truth,
　　And then for pardon pray?

My parents both are good and kind,
　　Though master is severe:
With weeping I am almost blind:
　　Oh! I shall perish here.

The night comes on, the air is sharp,
　　And now it blows a storm;
The pinching wind my skin doth warp,
　　My features soft deform.

As in the stream my face I viewed,
　　That face to me was new;
The buffetings of breezes rude
　　Have changed it black and blue.

My clothes are by the brambles torn,
　　My legs are wounded sore;
My friends to see my limbs would mourn,
　　These limbs all stained with gore.

I in some well or ditch may fall,
　　And there, when I am found,
Strangers will pity me, and all
　　Will say, 'The boy is drowned!'

This place is lonely, wild, and drear,
　　Nor stay the night I durst,
I'll lay me down and perish here,
　　With hunger and with thirst.

244

The Truant

I see a light ! a light 'tis plain !
  A Jack o' Lantern ? no !
It comes from yonder cottage pane,
  And to that cot I'll go.

No beggar-boy, alas ! am I :
  Oh give me shelter, pray ,
Or else with hunger I shall die,
  For I have lost my way.

Or on some straw, or on the floor,
  This night, oh ! let me lie ;
Or else the cold I must endure,
  Beneath this bitter sky.

And let me wash my face and feet ;
  Then give a little food ,
The plainest fare will be a treat,
  Dear woman, kind and good.

To-morrow morning take me home ;
  You'll hearty thanks receive :
My father's rich, though wild I roam,
  My tale you may believe.

If you should have a child distressed,
  My grief with pity see ,
With such a friend may he be blessed,
  As you shall pity me.

ADELAIDE.

RHYMES

FOR

THE NURSERY.

BY THE AUTHORS

OF

'ORIGINAL POEMS.'

LONDON:

Printed and sold by DARTON & HARVEY,
GRACECHURCH-STREET

1806.

Preface to the First Edition, 1806

IN the simple title of 'Rhymes for the Nursery' the pretensions of this little volume are fully explained. In the *Nursery* they are designed to circulate, and within its sanctuary walls the writers claim shelter from the eye of criticism ; though, should they appear to have admitted any *sentiment*, injudicious, erroneous, or dangerous, they ask not such an indulgence.

It has been questioned, by authority they respect, whether ideas adapted to the comprehension of infancy admit the restrictions of rhyme and metre? With humility, therefore, the present attempt has been made. Should it, however, in any degree prove successful, the writers must certainly acknowledge themselves indebted rather to the plainness of prose, than to the decorations of poetry.

RHYMES FOR THE NURSERY

(From the Edition of 1838)

The Cow

THANK you, pretty cow, that made
    Pleasant milk to soak my bread,
Every day, and every night,
Warm, and fresh, and sweet, and white.

Do not chew the hemlock rank,
Growing on the weedy bank;
But the yellow cowslips eat,
They will make it very sweet.

Where the purple violet grows,
Where the bubbling water flows,
Where the grass is fresh and fine,
Pretty cow, go there and dine.

Good Night

LITTLE baby, lay your head
  On your pretty cradle-bed ;
Shut your eye-peeps, now the day
And the light are gone away ;
All the clothes are tucked in tight ;
Little baby dear, good night.

Yes, my darling, well I know
How the bitter wind doth blow ;
And the winter's snow and rain,
Patter on the window-pane :
But they cannot come in here,
To my little baby dear ;

For the window shutteth fast,
Till the stormy night is past ;
And the curtains warm are spread
Round about her cradle-bed :
So till morning shineth bright
Little baby dear, good night.

'*Thank you, pretty cow*' (p. 251).

Getting Up

Getting Up

NOW, my baby, ope your eye,
 For the sun is in the sky,
And he's peeping once again
Through the frosty window-pane:
Little baby, do not keep
Any longer fast asleep.

There now, sit in mother's lap,
That she may untie your cap ;
For the little strings have got
Twisted into such a knot ·
Ah ! for shame, you've been at play
With the bobbin, as you lay.

There it comes, now let us see
Where your petticoats can be :
Oh ! they're in the window-seat,
Folded very smooth and neat .
When my baby older grows,
She shall double up her clothes

Now one pretty little kiss,
For dressing you so nice as this ;
And before we go down stairs,
Don't forget to say your prayers ,
For 'tis GOD who loves to keep
Little babies while they sleep.

Baby and Mamma

WHAT a little thing am I !
　　Hardly higher than the table :
I can eat, and play, and cry,
　　But to work I am not able.

Nothing in the world I know,
　　But mamma will try and show me :
Sweet mamma, I love her so,
　　She's so very kind unto me.

And she sets me on her knee,
　　Very often, for some kisses .
Oh ! how good I'll try to be,
　　For such a dear mamma as this is.

The Sparrows

HOP about, pretty sparrows, and pick up the
　　hay,
And the twigs, and the wool, and the moss ;
Indeed, I'll stand far enough out of your way,
　　Don't fly from the window so cross

I don't mean to catch you, you dear little Dick,
　　And fasten you up in a cage ;
To hop all day long on a straight bit of stick,
　　Or to flutter about in a rage.

I only just want to stand by you and see
　　How you gather the twigs for your house ;
Or sit at the foot of the jenneting tree,
　　While you twitter a song in the boughs.,

The Kind Mamma

Oh dear, if you'd eat a crumb out of my hand,
  How happy and glad I should be!
Then come, little bird, while I quietly stand
  At the foot of the jenneting tree.

The Kind Mamma

COME, dear, and sit upon my knee,
  And give me kisses, one, two, three
And tell me whether you love me,
        My baby.

For this I'm sure, that I love you,
And many, many things I do,
And all day long I sit and sew
        For baby.

And then at night I lie awake,
Thinking of things that I can make,
And trouble that I mean to take
        For baby.

And when you're good and do not cry,
Nor into naughty passions fly,
You can't think how papa and I
        Love baby.

But if my little child should grow,
To be a naughty child, you know
'Twould grieve mamma to see her so,
        My baby

And when you saw me pale and thin,
By grieving for my baby's sin,
I think you'd wish that you had been
        A better baby.

Learning to go Alone

COME, my darling, come away,
    Take a pretty walk to-day,
Run along, and never fear,
I'll take care of baby dear.
Up and down with little feet,
That's the way to walk, my sweet.
Now it is so very near,
Soon she'll get to mother dear.
There she comes along at last ·
Here's my finger, hold it fast:
Now one pretty little kiss,
After such a walk as this.

About the Little Girl that beat Her Sister

GO, go, my naughty girl, and kiss
    Your little sister dear,
I must not have such scenes as this,
    And noisy quarrels here.

What! little children scratch and fight
    That ought to be so mild,
Oh! Mary, it's a shocking sight
    To see an angry child.

I can't imagine, for my part,
    The reason of your folly,
She did not do you any harm,
    By playing with your dolly.

258

' *Run along, and never fear,*
I'll take care of baby dear.'

The Little Girl to Her Dolly

See, see, the little tears that run
    Fast from her watery eye:
Come, my sweet innocent, have done,
    'Twill do no good to cry.

Go, Mary, wipe her tears away,
    And make it up with kisses.
And never turn a pretty play
    To such a pet as this is.

The Little Girl to Her Dolly

THERE, go to sleep, Dolly, in own mother's lap;
    I've put on your night-gown and neat little
    cap,
So sleep, pretty baby, and shut up your eye,
Bye bye, little Dolly, lie still and bye bye.

I'll lay my clean handkerchief over your head,
And then make believe that my lap is your bed,
So hush, little dear, and be sure you don't cry ·
Bye bye, little Dolly, lie still, and bye bye.

There, now it is morning, and time to get up,
And I'll crumb you a mess in my own china cup;
So wake, little baby, and open your eye,
For I think it's high time to have done with bye bye.

The Star

TWINKLE, twinkle, little star,
How I wonder what you are!
Up above the world so high,
Like a diamond in the sky.

When the blazing sun is gone,
When he nothing shines upon,
Then you show your little light,
Twinkle, twinkle, all the night.

Then the traveller in the dark,
Thanks you for your tiny spark!
He could not see which way to go,
If you did not twinkle so.

In the dark blue sky you keep,
And often through my curtains peep,
For you never shut your eye
Till the sun is in the sky.

As your bright and tiny spark
Lights the traveller in the dark,
Though I know not what you are,
Twinkle, twinkle, little star.

Come and play in the Garden

LITTLE sister, come away,
And let us in the garden play,
For it is a pleasant day.

On the grass-plot let us sit,
Or, if you please, we'll play a bit,
And run about all over it.

But the fruit we will not pick,
For that would be a naughty trick,
And very likely make us sick.

Nor will we pluck the pretty flowers
That grow about the beds and bowers,
Because you know they are not ours. .

We'll take the daisies, white and red,
Because mamma has often said,
That we may gather them instead.

And much I hope we always may
Our very dear mamma obey,
And mind whatever she may say.

About learning to Read

HERE'S a pretty gay book, full of verses to sing,
But Lucy can't read it; oh! what a sad thing!
And such funny stories—and pictures too—look:
I am glad I can read such a beautiful book.

But come, little Lucy, now what do you say,
Shall I begin teaching you pretty great A?
And then all the letters that stand in a row,
That you may be able to read it, you know?

A great many children have no kind mamma,
To teach them to read, and poor children they are!
But Lucy shall learn all her letters to tell,
And I hope by and bye she will read very well.

No Breakfast for Growler

'NO, naughty Growler, get away,
You shall not have a bit,
Now when I speak, how dare you stay?
I can't spare any, Sir, I say,
And so you need not sit.'

Poor Growler! do not make him go,
But recollect, before,
That he has never served you so,
For you have given him many a blow,
That patiently he bore.

Poor Growler! if he could but speak,
He'd tell (as well he might)
How he would bear with many a freak,
And wag his tail, and look so meek,
And neither bark nor bite.

" ' " No, naughty Growler, get away,
You shall not have a bit." ' "

Poor Children

Upon his back he lets you ride,
 All round and round the yard ;
And now, while sitting by your side,
To have a bit of bread denied,
 Is really very hard.

And all your little tricks he'll bear,
 And never seem to mind,
And yet you say you cannot spare
One bit of breakfast for his share,
 Although he is so kind !

Poor Children

WHEN I go in the meadows, or walk in the street,
 How many poor children I frequently meet,
Without shoes or stockings to cover their feet.

Their clothes are all ragged and let in the cold ;
And they have so little to eat I am told,
That indeed 'tis a pitiful sight to behold !

And then I have seen, very often, that they
Are cross and unkind to each other at play ;
But they've not been taught better, I've heard mamma
 say

But I have kind parents to watch over me,
To teach me how gentle and good I should be,
And to mourn for the poor little children I see.

Learning to Draw

COME, here are a slate, and a pencil, and string,
   So let us sit down and draw some pretty thing;
A man, and a cow, and a horse, and a tree,
And when you have finished, pray show them to me.

What! cannot you do it? Shall I show you how?
Come, give me your pencil, I'll draw you a cow.
You've made the poor creature look very forlorn!
She has but three legs, dear, and only one horn.

Now see, I have drawn you a beautiful cow;
And here is a dicky-bird, perched on a bough,
And here are some more flying down from above:
There now, is not that very pretty, my love?

Oh yes, very pretty! now make me some more,
A house with a gate, and a window, and door,
And a little boy flying his kite with a string,
For you know, dear mamma, you can draw any thing.

Of what are Your Clothes made?

COME here to papa, and I'll tell my dear boy,
  (For I think he would never have guessed),
How many poor animals we must employ
  Before little Charles can be dressed.

The pretty Sheep gives you the wool from his sides,
  To make you a jacket to use;
And the Dog or the Seal must be stripp'd of their hides,
  To give you these nice little shoes.

And then the shy Beaver contributes his share
  With the Rabbit, to give you a hat;
For this must be made of their delicate hair,
  And so you may thank them for that.

All these I have mentioned, and many more too,
  Each willingly gives us a share,
One sends us a hat and another a shoe,
  That we may have plenty to wear.

Then as the poor creatures are suffered to give
  So much for the comfort of man,
I think 'tis but right, that as long as they live
  We should do all for them that we can.

Little Girls must not Fret

WHAT is it that makes little Emily cry?
    Come then, let mamma wipe the tear from
    her eye:
There—lay down your head on my bosom—that's right,
And now tell mamma what's the matter to-night.

What! Emmy is sleepy, and tired with play?
Come, Betty, make haste then, and fetch her away;
But do not be fretful, my darling, because
Mamma cannot love little girls that are cross.

She shall soon go to bed and forget it all there.
Ah! here's her sweet smile come again, I declare:
That's right, for I thought you quite naughty before:
Good night, my dear child, but don't fret any more.

Breakfast and Puss

HERE'S my baby's bread and milk,
    For her lip as soft as silk,
Here's the basin clean and neat,
Here's the spoon of silver sweet,
Here's the stool, and here's the chair,
For my little lady fair.

No, you must not spill it out,
And drop the bread and milk about;
But let it stand before you flat,
And pray remember pussy-cat:
Poor old pussy-cat, that purrs
All so patiently for hers.

270

The Flower and the Lady

True, she runs about the house,
Catching now and then a mouse;
But, though she thinks it very. nice,
That only makes a tiny slice ·
So don't forget that you should stop,
And leave poor puss a little drop

The Flower and the Lady, about Getting Up

PRETTY flower, tell me why
    All your leaves do open wide,
Every morning, when on high
    The noble sun begins to ride.

This is why, my lady fair,
    If you would the reason know,
For betimes the pleasant air
    Very cheerfully doth blow.

And the birds on every tree,
    Sing a merry, merry tune,
And the busy honey-bee
    Comes to suck my sugar soon.

This is, then, the reason why
    I my little leaves undo :
Little lady, wake and try
    If I have not told you true.

The Baby's Dance

DANCE, little baby, dance up high :
Never mind, baby, mother is by ,
Crow and caper, caper and crow,
There, little baby, there you go ;
Up to the ceiling, down to the ground,
Backwards and forwards, round and round ·
Then dance, little baby, and mother shall sing,
While the gay merry coral goes ding, ding-a-ding,
    ding.

For a Little Girl that did not Like
to be Washed

WHAT ! cry when I wash you, not love to be
    clean !
Then go and be dirty, not fit to be seen
And till you leave off, and I see you have smiled,
I can't take the trouble to wash such a child.

Suppose I should leave you now just as you are,
Do you think you'd deserve a sweet kiss from papa,
Or to sit on his knee and learn pretty great A,
With fingers that have not been washed all the day ?

Ay, look at your fingers, you see it is so
Did you ever behold such a black little row ?
And for once you may look at yourself in the glass ;
There's a face to belong to a good little lass !
Come, come then, I see you're beginning to clear,
You won't be so foolish again, will you, dear ?

'*Dance, little baby, dance up high.*'

The Cut

WELL, what's the matter? there's a face!
    What! have you cut a vein?
And it is quite a shocking place!
    Come, let us look again.

I see it bleeds, but never mind
    That tiny little drop;
I don't believe you'll ever find
    That crying makes it stop.

'Tis sad indeed to cry at pain,
    For any but a baby;
If that should chance to cut a vein,
    We should not wonder, may be.

But such a man as you should try
    To bear a little sorrow:
So run about and wipe your eye,
    'Twill all be well to-morrow.

275

The Little Girl that Could not Read

I DON'T know my letters, and what shall I do?
For I've got a nice book, but I can't read it
through!
Oh dear how I wish that my letters I knew!

I think I had better begin them to-day,
'Tis so like a dunce to be always at play·
Mamma, if you please, will you teach me great A?

And then B and C, as they stand in the row,
One after another, as far as they go,
For then I can read my new story, you know.

So pray, mamma, teach me at once, and you'll see
What a good—very good little child I shall be,
To try and remember my A, B, C, D.

Questions and Answers

WHO showed the little ant the way
Her narrow hole to bore,
And spend the pleasant summer day,
In laying up her store?

The sparrow builds her clever nest,
Of wool, and hay, and moss
Who told her how to weave it best,
And lay the twigs across?

Who taught the busy bee to fly
Among the sweetest flowers,
And lay his feast of honey by,
To eat in winter hours?

Playing with Fire

'Twas God who showed them all the way,
  And gave their little skill,
And teaches children, if they pray,
  To do His holy will.

Playing with Fire

' I 'VE seen a little girl, mamma !
    That had got such a dreadful scar !
All down her arms, and neck, and face,
I could not bear to see the place.'

' Poor little girl, and don't you know
  The shocking trick that made her so ?
'Twas all because she went and did
  A thing her mother had forbid.

' For once, when nobody was by her,
  This silly child would play with fire ;
And long before her mother came,
  Her pinafore was all in flame

' In vain she tried to put it out,
  Till all her clothes were burnt about :
And then she suffered ten times more,
  All over with a dreadful sore :

' For many months before 'twas cured,
  Most shocking tortures she endured ;
And even now, in passing by her,
  You see what 'tis to play with fire !'

The Field Daisy

I 'M a pretty little thing,
  Always coming with the spring ;
In the meadows green I'm found,
Peeping just above the ground,
And my stalk is covered flat,
With a white and yellow hat.

Little Mary, when you pass
Lightly o'er the tender grass,
Skip about, but do not tread
On my bright but lowly head,
For I always seem to say,
' Surly winter's gone away.'

The Michaelmas Daisy

I AM very pale and dim,
  With my faint and bluish rim,
Standing on my narrow stalk,
By the littered gravel walk,
And the withered leaves aloft,
Fall upon me very oft.

But I show my lonely head
When the other flowers are dead,
And you're even glad to spy
Such a homely thing as I ,
For I seem to smile and say,
' Summer is not quite away.'

Dutiful Jem

THERE was a poor widow, who lived in a cot,
  She scarcely a blanket to warm her had got;
Her windows were broken, her walls were all bare,
And the cold winter-wind often whistled in there.

Poor Susan was old, and too feeble to spin,
Her forehead was wrinkled, her hands they were thin,
And bread she'd have wanted, as many have done,
If she had not been blessed with a good little son.

But he loved her well, like a dutiful lad,
And thought her the very best friend that he had:
And now to neglect or forsake her, he knew,
Was the most wicked thing he could possibly do.

For he was quite healthy, and active, and stout,
While his poor mother hardly could hobble about,
And he thought it his duty and greatest delight,
To work for her living from morning to night.

So he started each morning as gay as a lark,
And worked all day long in the fields till 'twas dark:
Then came home again to his dear mother's cot,
And cheerfully gave her the wages he got.

And oh, how she loved him! how great was her joy!
To think her dear Jem was a dutiful boy.
Her arm round his neck she would tenderly cast,
And kiss his red cheek, while the tears trickled fast.

Oh, then, was not this little Jem happier far
Than naughty, and idle, and foolish boys are?
For, as long as he lived, 'twas his comfort and joy,
To think he'd not been an undutiful boy.

The Ant's Nest

IT is such a beautiful day,
　And the sun shines so bright and so warm,
That the little ants, busy and gay,
　Are come from their holes in a swarm.

All the winter together they sleep,
　Or in underground passages run,
Not one of them daring to peep,
　To see the bright face of the sun.

But the snow is now melted away,
　And the trees are all covered with green ;
And these little ants, busy and gay,
　Creeping out from their houses are seen.

They've left us no room to go by,
　So we'll step aside on to the grass,
For a hundred poor insects might die
　Under your little feet as they pass.

Sleepy Harry

' I DO not like to go to bed,'
   Sleepy little Harry said,
' Go, naughty Betty, go away,
I will not come at all, I say !'

Oh, what a silly little fellow !
I should be quite ashamed to tell her ;
Then, Betty, you must come and carry
This very foolish little Harry.

The little birds are better taught,
They go to roosting when they ought;
And all the ducks and fowls, you know,
They went to bed an hour ago.

The little beggar in the street,
Who wanders with his naked feet,
And has not where to lay his head,
Oh, he'd be glad to go to bed.

Going to Bed

DOWN upon my pillow warm,
　　I do lay my little head,
And the rain, and wind, and storm,
　　Cannot come too nigh my bed.

Many little children poor
　　Have not any where to go,
And sad hardships they endure,
　　Such as I did never know.

Dear mamma, I'll thank you oft
　　For this comfortable bed,
And this pretty pillow soft,
　　Where I rest my little head.

I shall sleep till morning light,
　　On a bed so nice as this;
So my dear mamma, good night,
　　Give your little girl a kiss.

'Many little children poor
Have not anywhere to go.'

Idle Mary

OH, Mary, this will never do!
   This work is sadly done, my dear,
And then so little of it too!
   You have not taken pains, I fear.

Oh no, your work has been forgotten,
   Indeed you've hardly thought of that;
I saw you roll your ball of cotton
   About the floor to please the cat.

See, here are stitches straggling wide,
   And others reaching down so far;
I'm very sure you have not tried
   In this, at least, to please mamma.

The little girl who will not sew
   Should neither be allowed to play;
But then I hope, my love, that you
   Will take more pains another day.

The Little Husbandman

I'M a little husbandman,
　　Work and labour hard I can:
I am as happy all the day
At my work as if 'twere play:
Though I've nothing fine to wear,
Yet for that I do not care.

When to work I go along,
Singing loud my morning song,
With my wallet at my back,
Or my waggon-whip to smack;
Oh! I am as happy then
As any idle gentlemen.

I've a hearty appetite,
And I soundly sleep at night,
Down I lie content, and say,
'I've been useful all the day:
I'd rather be a plough-boy than
A useless little gentleman.'

'I'm a little husbandman.'

The Little Child

I'M a very little child,
  Only just have learned to speak
So I should be very mild,
  Very tractable and meek.

If my dear mamma were gone,
  I should perish soon, and die,
When she left me all alone,
  Such a little thing as I !

Oh, what service can I do,
  To repay her for her care ?
For I cannot even sew,
  Nor make any thing I wear.

Oh then, I will always try
  To be very good and mild ;
Never now be cross or cry,
  Like a fretful little child

For sometimes I cry and fret,
  And my dear mamma I tease ;
Or I vex her, while I sit
  Playing pretty on her knees.

Oh, how can I serve her so,
  Such a good mamma as this !
Round her neck my arms I'll throw,
  And her gentle cheeks I'll kiss.

Then I'll tell her, that I will
  Try not any more to fret her,
And as I grow older still,
  Try to show I love her better.

x

The Old Beggar Man

I SEE an old man sitting there,
His withered limbs are almost bare,
And very hoary is his hair.

Old man, why are you sitting so?
For very cold the wind doth blow:
Why don't you to your cottage go?

Ah, master, in the world so wide,
I have no home wherein to hide,
No comfortable fire-side.

When I, like you, was young and gay,
I'll tell you what I used to say,—
That I would nothing do but play.

And so, instead of being taught
Some useful business as I ought,
To play about was all I sought.

And now that I am old and grey,
I wander on my lonely way,
And beg my bread from day to day.

But oft I shake my hoary head,
And many a bitter tear I shed,
To think the useless life I've led.

The Little Coward

WHY, here's a foolish little man,
  Laugh at him, donkey, if you can,
And cat, and dog, and cow, and calf,
Come every one of you and laugh.

For only think, he runs away
If honest donkey does but bray!
And when the bull begins to bellow,
He's like a crazy little fellow.

Poor Brindle cow can hardly pass
Along the hedge, to nip the grass,
Or wag her tail to lash the flies,
But off he runs, and loudly cries!

And when old Tray comes jumping too,
With bow, wow, wow, for how d'ye do,
And means it all for civil play,
'Tis sure to make him run away!

But all the while you're thinking, may be
'Ah! well, but this must be a baby.'
Oh! cat, and dog, and cow, and calf,
I'm not surprised to see you laugh,
He's five years old and almost half.

The Sheep

'LAZY sheep, pray tell me why
 In the pleasant fields you lie,
Eating grass and daisies white,
From the morning till the night?
Every thing can something do,
But what kind of use are you?'

'Nay, my little master, nay,
 Do not serve me so, I pray :
Don't you see the wool that grows
On my back, to make you clothes?
Cold, and very cold, you'd be,
If you had not wool from me.

'True, it seems a pleasant thing,
 To nip the daisies in the spring ;
But many chilly nights I pass
On the cold and dewy grass,
Or pick a scanty dinner, where
All the common's brown and bare

'Then the farmer comes at last,
 When the merry spring is past,
And cuts my woolly coat away,
To warm you in the winter's day :
Little master, this is why
In the pleasant fields I lie.'

The Little Boy who Made Himself Ill

' AH ! why is my sweet little fellow so pale ?
And why do these briny tears fall ?
Come to me, love, and tell me what is it you ail,
And we'll soon try to cure him of all.

' There, lay your white cheek down on own mother's la
With your pinafore over your head,
And perhaps we shall see, when you've taken a nap,
That this pale little cheek may be red '

' Oh ! no, dear mamma, don't be kind to me yet,
I do not deserve to be kissed ;
Last evening some gooseberries and currants I ate,
For I thought that they would not be missed.

' And so, when in the garden you left me alone,
I took them, although they were green,
But I thought, dear mamma, 'twould be better to ow
What a sad naughty boy I have been.'

' Indeed, my dear child, I am sorry to hear
This very wrong thing you have done,
Twas not only eating the fruit when unripe,
But taking what was not your own ;

' And now you must patiently bear with the pain,
That does your own folly repay,
And I hope you will not be so naughty again,
After all you have suffered to day !'

293

To a Little Girl that liked to look in the Glass

WHAT ! looking in the glass again !
Why is my silly girl so vain?
Do you think yourself as fair
As the gentle lilies are ?

Is your merry eye so blue
As the violet, wet with dew ?
Yet it loves the best to hide
By the hedge's shady side.

When your cheek the brightest glows,
Is it redder than the rose ?
But the rose's buds are seen
Almost hid with moss and green.

Little flowers that open gay,
Peeping forth at break of day,
In the garden, hedge, or plain,
Do you think that they are vain ?

'What! looking in the glass again!'

The Cruel Boy and the Kittens

WHAT! go to see the kittens drowned,
   On purpose, in the yard!
I did not think there could be found
   A little heart so hard.

Poor kittens! no more pretty play
   With pussy's wagging tail:
Oh! I'd go far enough away,
   Before I'd see the pail.

Poor things! the little child that can
   Be pleased to go and see,
Most likely, when he grows a man,
   A cruel man will be.

And many a wicked thing he'll do,
   Because his heart is hard;
A great deal worse than killing you,
   Poor kittens, in the yard.

The Work-Bag

COME here, I've got a piece of rag,
    To make you quite a pretty bag ;
Indeed you will not often see
As nice a bag as this shall be.

And when it's done, I'll show you, too,
The other things I have for you ;
This book's to put your needles in,
And that you know's a pincushion.

And then, you need not lose a minute,
But if you always keep them in it,
You never more will need to say,
' Where ever are my things to-day ?

' Pray, somebody, do try and look,
To find my pin and needle-book ':
But then the pleasant sound shall be ;—
' They're in my work-bag, I shall see !'

Which is the Best Way to be Happy?

I THINK I should like to be happy to-day,
If I could but tell which was the easiest way:
But then, I don't know any pretty new play:

And as to the old ones—why which is the best?
There's fine blind-man's-buff, hide-and-seek, and the rest
Or pretending it's tea-time, when dollies are dress'd!

But no—let me see, now I've thought of a way,
Which would really I think be still better than play,
I'll try to be good, if I can, the whole day.

Without any fretting or crying: oh, no,
For that makes me unhappy wherever I go,
And it would be a pity to spoil the day so.

I don't choose to be such a baby, not I,
To be peevish and cross and just ready to cry:
And mamma 'll be so pleased, that at least I will try!

The Frolicsome Kitten

'DEAR kitten, do lie still, I say,
    I really want you to be quiet,
Instead of scampering away,
    And always making such a riot.

'There, only see! you've torn my frock,
    And poor mamma must put a patch in;
I'll give you a right earnest knock,
    To cure you of this trick of scratching.'

Nay, do not scold your little cat,
    She does not know what 'tis you're saying;
And every time you give a pat,
    She thinks you mean it all for playing.

But if poor pussy understood
    The lesson that you want to teach her,
And did not choose to be so good,
    She'd be, indeed, a naughty creature.

A Fine Thing

A Fine Thing

WHO am I with noble face,
  Shining in a clear blue place?
If to look at me you try,
I shall blind your little eye.

When my noble face I shew,
Over yonder mountain blue,
All the clouds away do ride,
And the dusky night beside.

Then the clear wet dews I dry,
With the look of my bright eye;
And the little birds awake,
Many a merry tune to make.

Cowslips, then, and hare-bells blue,
And lily-cups their leaves undo,
For they shut themselves up tight,
All the dark and foggy night.

Then the busy people go,
Some to plough, and some to sow;
When I leave, their work is done;
Guess, if I am not the Sun.

A Pretty Thing

WHO am I that shine so bright,
With my pretty yellow light,
Peeping through your curtains grey ?
Tell me, little girl, I pray.

When the sun is gone, I rise,
In the very silent skies ,
And a cloud or two doth skim
Round about my silver rim.

All the little stars do seem
Hidden by my brighter beam ;
And among them I do ride,
Like a queen in all her pride.

Then the reaper goes along,
Singing forth a merry song,
While I light the shaking leaves,
And the yellow harvest sheaves.

Little girl, consider well,
Who this simple tale doth tell ;
And I think you'll guess it soon,
For I only am the Moon.

Little Birds and Cruel Boys

A LITTLE bird built a warm nest in a tree,
  And laid some blue eggs in it, one, two, and
      three,
And then very glad and delighted was she.

And after a while, but how long I can't tell,
The little ones crept, one by one, from the shell;
And their mother was pleased, for she loved them all
    well.

She spread her soft wings on them all the day long,
To warm and to guard them, her love was so strong;
And her mate sat beside her, and sung her a song.

One day the young birds were all crying for food,
So off flew their mother away from her brood,
And up came some boys, who were wicked and rude.

So they pull'd the warm nest down away from the tree·
And the little ones cried, but they could not get free,
So at last they all died away, one, two, and three.

But when back to the nest the poor mother did fly,
Oh, then she set up a most pitiful cry!
And she mourned a long while, and then lay down to die!

The Snowdrop

NOW the spring is coming on,
    Now the snow and ice are gone,
Come, my little snowdrop root,
Will you not begin to shoot?

Ah! I see your pretty head
Peeping on the flower-bed,
Looking all so green and gay
On this fine and pleasant day.

For the mild south wind doth blow,
And hath melted all the snow,
And the sun shines out so warm,
You need not fear another storm.

So your pretty flower show,
And your petals white undo,
Then you'll hang your modest head
Down upon my flower bed.

Romping

WHY now, my dear boys, this is always the way,
You can't be contented with innocent play,
But this sort of romping, so noisy and high,
Is never left off till it ends in a cry.

What! are there no games you can take a delight in,
But kicking, and knocking, and tearing, and fighting?
It is a sad thing to be forced to conclude
That boys can't be merry, without being rude.

Now what is the reason you never can play,
Without snatching each other's playthings away?
It can be no hardship to let them alone,
When each of you has such nice toys of his own?

I often have told you before, my dear boys,
That I do not object to your making a noise;
Or running and jumping about, any how,
But fighting and mischief I cannot allow.

So, if any more of these quarrels are heard,
I tell you this once, and I'll keep to my word,
I'll take every marble, and spin-top, and ball,
And not let you play with each other at all.

Working

WELL, now I'll sit down, and I'll work very
    fast,
And try if I can't be a good girl at last:
'Tis better than being so sulky and haughty,
I'm really quite tired of being so naughty.

For, as mamma says, when my business is done,
There's plenty of time left to play and to run:
But when 'tis my work-time I ought to sit still,
And I know that I ought, so I certainly will.

But for fear, after all, I should get at my play,
I will put my wax-doll in the closet away;
And I'll not look to see what the kitten is doing,
Nor yet think of any thing else but my sewing.

I'm sorry I've idled so often before,
But I hope I shall never do so any more:
Mamma will be pleased when she sees how I mend,
And have done this long seam from beginning to end!

The Selfish Snails

IT happened that a little snail
　　Came crawling, with his slimy tail,
　Upon a cabbage-stalk;
But two more little snails were there,
Both feasting on this dainty fare,
　Engaged in friendly talk.

' No, no, you shall not dine with us;
How dare you interrupt us thus?'
　The greedy snails declare;
So their poor brother they discard,
Who really thinks it very hard
　He may not have his share.

But selfish folks are sure to know
They get no good by being so,
　In earnest or in play;
Which these two snails confessed, no doubt,
When soon the gardener spied them out,
　And threw them both away.

Good Dobbin

OH! thank you, good Dobbin, you've been a long
     track,
And have carried papa all the way on your back;
You shall have some nice oats, faithful Dobbin, indeed,
For you've brought papa home to his darling with speed.

The howling wind blew, and the pelting rain beat,
And the thick mud has covered his legs and his feet,
But yet on he galloped in spite of the rain,
And has brought papa home to his darling again.

The sun it was setting a long while ago,
And papa could not see the road where he should go,
But Dobbin kept on through the desolate wild,
And has brought papa home to his dear little child.

Now go to the stable, the night is so raw,
Go, Dobbin, and rest your old bones on the straw:
Don't stand any longer out here in the rain,
For you've brought papa home to his darling again.

Sulking

Sulking

WHY is Mary standing there,
Leaning down upon a chair,
With such an angry lip and brow?
I wonder what's the matter now.

Come here, my dear, and tell me true,
Is it because I spoke to you
About the work you'd done so slow,
That you are standing fretting so?

Why, then, indeed, I'm grieved to see
That you can so ill-tempered be;
You make your fault a great deal worse,
By being angry and perverse

Oh, how much better 'twould appear
To see you shed a humble tear,
And then to hear you meekly say,
' I'll not do so another day.'

For you to stand and look so cross
(Which makes your fault so much the worse)
Is far more naughty, dear, you know,
Than having done your work so slow!

Time to go to Bed

THE sun at evening sets, and then
    The lion leaves his gloomy den ;
He roars along the forest wide,
Till all who hear are terrified :
There he prowls at evening hour,
Seeking something to devour.

When the sun is in the west,
The white owl leaves his darksome nest ;
Wide he opes his staring eyes,
And screams, as round and round he flies ;
For he hates the cheerful light,
He sleeps by day, and wakes at night.

When the lion cometh out,
When the white owl flies about,
I must lay my sleepy head
Down upon my pleasant bed ;
There all night I'll lay me still,
While the owl is screaming shrill.

Time to get Up

THE cock, who soundly sleeps at night,
Rises with the morning light,
Very loud and shrill he crows;
Then the sleeping ploughman knows
He must leave his bed also,
To his morning work to go.

And the little lark does fly
To the middle of the sky:
You may hear his merry tune,
In the morning very soon;
For he does not like to rest
Idly in his downy nest.

While the cock is crowing shrill,
Leave my little bed I will,
And I'll rise to hear the lark,
Now it is no longer dark:
'Twould be a pity there to stay,
When 'tis bright and pleasant day.

The Poor Fly

'SO, so, you are running away, Mr. Fly,
    But I'll come at you now, if you don't go too high ;
There, there, I have caught you, you can't get away :
Never mind, my old fellow, I'm only in play.'

Oh Charles ! cruel Charles ! you have killed the poor fly,
You have pinched him so hard, he is going to die :
His legs are all broken, and he cannot stand ;
There, now he has fallen down dead from your hand !

I hope you are sorry for what you have done ·
You may *kill* many flies, but you cannot *make* one.
No, you can't set it up, as I told you before,
It is dead, and it never will stand any more.

Poor thing ! as it buzzed up and down on the glass,
How little it thought what was coming to pass !
For it could not have guessed, as it frisked in the sun,
That a child would destroy it for nothing but fun.

The spider, who weaves his fine cobweb so neat,
Might have caught him, indeed, for he wants him to eat ;
But the poor flies must learn to keep out of your way,
As you kill them for nothing at all but your play.

The Tumble

TUMBLE down, tumble up, never mind it, my
    sweet ;
No, no, never beat the poor floor :
'Twas your fault, that could not stand straight on your
    feet,
    Beat yourself, if you beat any more.

Oh dear ! what a noise : will a noise make it well?
    Will crying wash bruises away ?
Suppose that it should bleed a little and swell,
    'Twill all be gone down in a day.

That's right, be a man, love, and dry up your tears.
    Come, smile, and I'll give you a kiss :
If you live in the world but a very few years,
    You must bear greater troubles than this.

Ah ! there's the last tear dropping down from your
    cheek !
    All the dimples are coming again !
And your round little face looks as ruddy and meek
    As a rose that's been washed in the rain.

313

The Little Fish that would not do as it was bid

'DEAR mother,' said a little fish.
  'Pray is not that a fly?
I'm very hungry, and I wish
  You'd let me go and try.'

'Sweet innocent,' the mother cried,
  And started from her nook,
'That horrid fly is put to hide
  , The sharpness of the hook.'

Now, as I've heard, this little trout
  Was young and foolish too,
And so he thought he'd venture out,
  To see if it were true.

And round about the hook he played,
  With many a longing look,
And—'Dear me,' to himself he said,
  'I'm sure that's not a hook.

'I can but give one little pluck:
  Let's see, and so I will.'
So on he went, and lo! it stuck
  Quite through his little gill

And as he faint and fainter grew,
  With hollow voice he cried,
'Dear mother, had I minded you,
  I need not now have died'

The Little Baby

WHAT is this pretty little thing,
    That nurse so carefully doth bring,
And round its head her apron fling ?
        A baby !

Oh ! dear, how very soft its cheek ,
Why, nurse, I cannot make it speak,
And it can't walk, it is so weak,
        Poor baby.

Here, take a bit, you little dear,
I've got some cake and sweetmeats here :
'Tis very nice, you need not fear,
        You baby.

Oh ! I'm afraid that it will die,
Why can't it eat as well as I,
And jump and talk ? Do let it try,
        Poor baby.

Why, you were once a baby too,
But could not jump as now you do,
But good mamma took care of you,
        Like baby.

And then she taught your pretty feet
To pat along the carpet neat,
And called papa to come and meet
        His baby.

Oh ! dear mamma, to take such care,
And no kind pains and trouble spare,
To feed and nurse you, when you were
        A baby.

What came of firing a Gun

AH ! there it falls, and now it's dead,
  The shot went through its pretty head,
And broke its shining wing !
How dull and dim its closing eyes !
How cold and stiff, and still it lies !
  Poor harmless little thing !

It was a lark, and in the sky,
In mornings fine, it mounted high,
  To sing a merry song :
Cutting the fresh and healthy air,
It whistled out its music there,
  As light it skimmed along.

How little thought its pretty breast,
This morning, when it left its nest
  Hid in the springing corn,
To find some breakfast for its young,
And pipe away its morning song—
  It never should return

Those pretty wings shall never more
Its callow nestlings cover o'er,
  Or bring them dainties rare :
But long their gaping beaks will cry,
And then they will with hunger die,
  All in the bitter air.

Poor little bird ! if people knew
The sorrows little birds go through,
  I think that even boys
Would never call it sport or fun,
To stand and fire a frightful gun,
  For nothing but the noise.

The Little Negro

The Little Negro

AH! the poor little blackamore, see there he goes,
How the blood gushes out from his half-frozen
toes,
And his legs are so thin you may almost see the bones,
As he goes shiver, shiver, all along upon the stones.

He was once a negro boy, and a merry boy was he,
With the other little negroes by the tall palm-tree,
Or bathing in the river like a brisk water-rat,
And at night sleeping sound on his little piece of mat.

But there came some wicked people, and they stole him
far away,
And then good-bye to the tall palm-tree, and all his merry
play ;
For they took him from his house and home, and everybody dear,
And now, poor little negro boy, he's come a begging
here.

Oh, fie upon those wicked men who did this cruel thing !
I wish some mighty nobleman would go and tell the
king ;
For to steal him from his house and home must be a
crying sin,
Though he was a little negro boy and had a sooty skin.

About the Little Negro again

I 'VE heard a pretty story, and I'll tell it you, my
dear ;
'Tis true as well as beautiful, and does one good to hear ;
About the little negro boy, and many, many, more ;
But not about the cruel things that I told you of before.

For thousands upon thousands of good people in the
land,
Did write such pretty letters, that the king might understand,
And sent them up to Parliament, to beg that they would
do—
As Jesus Christ had told them—' as they would be done
unto.'

They prayed them just to make a law, that no such
thing might be,
But everybody, white or black, should after that be free :
For God had made us all alike, and all to Him belong ;
And stealing men and women we are certain must be
wrong.

So on the first of August, eighteen hundred thirty-four,
We told the poor black people, we would serve them so
no more ;
We ' did as we'd be done unto,'—which is so very clear ,
And that's the pleasant story, which it does one good to
hear.

Poor Donkey

POOR Donkey, I'll give him a handful of grass,
 i'm sure he's a good-natured, honest old ass :
He trots to the market to carry the sack,
And lets me ride all the way home on his back ;
And only just stops by the ditch for a minute,
To see if there's any fresh grass for him in it.

'Tis true, now and then, he has got a bad trick
Of standing stock still, or e'en trying to kick ;
And then, poor old fellow, you know, he can't tell
That standing stock still is not using me well ;
For it never comes into his head, I dare say,
To do his work first, and then afterwards play.

No, no, my good Donkey, I'll give you some grass,
For you know no better, because you're an ass ;
But what little donkeys some children must look,
Who stand, just as you do, stock still at their book !
For to waste every moment of time as it passes,
Is being more stupid and silly than asses.

The Spring Nosegay

COME, my love, 'tis pleasant spring,
   Let us make a posy gay,
Every pretty flower we'll bring,
   Which we'll gather while we may.
Here's Hepatica so blue,
Holding little drops of dew !

There's the Snow-drop, hanging low,
   On its green and narrow stalk ;
And the Crocuses that blow
   Up and down the garden walk ;
Will the Polyanthus say,
These must all be ours to-day !

After that the Primrose fair,
   Looking sweetly pale and dim ;
And we'll search the meadows, where
   Cowslips show their yellow rim ;
Then along the hedge we'll go,
Where the early Violets blow ;
All these pretty flowers we'll bring,
To make our posy for the spring !

The Summer Nosegay

NOW the yellow Cowslips fade,
   All along the woody walk ;
And the Primrose hangs her head
   Faintly, on her tiny stalk ;
Let us to the garden go,
Where the flowers of summer grow.

Come, and make a nosegay there,
   Plucking every flower that blows :
Briar sweet, and Lily fair,
   That along the valley grows ;
With a Honey-suckle red,
Round the shady arbour led.

Then a budding Rose or two,
   Half in mossy leaves enrolled,
With the Larkspur, red and blue,
   Streaky Pink, and Marigold :
These shall make our posy gay,
For the cheerful summer day.

The Autumn Nosegay

NOW the fog has risen high,
    Through the chilly morning air;
And the blue and cheerful sky
    Peeps upon us, here and there ,
Once again we'll gather, sweet,
Every pretty flower we meet.

Ah ! the yellow leaves are now
    Over all the garden spread,
Showered down from every bough
    On the lonely flower-bed ,
Where the autumn Daisy blue
Opens, wet with chilly dew

Lavender, of darksome green,
    Shows its purple blossoms near :
And the Golden-rod is seen,
    Shooting up its yellow spear ;
These are all that we can find,
In our posy gay to bind.

The Winter Nosegay

NOW the winds of winter blow
  Fiercely through the chilly air ;
Now the fields are white with snow,
  Can we find a posy there ?
No, there cannot, all around,
A single blade of grass be found.

Nothing but the Holly bright,
  Spotted with its berries gay ;
Lauristinus, red and white,
  Or the Ivy's crooked spray ;
With a Sloe of darksome blue,
Where the ragged Blackthorn grew.

Or the Hip of shining red,
  Where the wild Rose used to blow,
Peeping out its scarlet head,
  From beneath a cap of snow.
These are all that dare to stay,
Through the cutting winter's day.

The Little Lark

I HEAR a pretty bird, but hark!
  I cannot see it anywhere.
Oh! it is a little lark,
  Singing in the morning air.
Little lark, do tell me why
You are singing in the sky?

Other little birds at rest,
  Have not yet begun to sing,
Every one is in its nest,
  With its head behind its wing.
Little lark, then, tell me why
You're so early in the sky?

You look no bigger than a bee,
  In the middle of the blue;
Up above the poplar tree,
  I can hardly look at you.
Little lark, do tell me why
You are mounted up so high?

'Tis to watch the silver star,
  Sinking slowly in the skies;
And beyond the mountain far,
  See the glorious sun arise.
Little lady, this is why
I am mounted up so high.

'Tis to sing a merry song
  To the pleasant morning light,
Why stay in my nest so long,
  When the sun is shining bright?
Little lady, this is why
I sing so early in the sky.

The Quarrelsome Dogs

To the little birds below,
I do sing a merry tune;
And I let the ploughman know
He must come to labour soon.
Little lady, this is why
I am singing in the sky.

The Quarrelsome Dogs

OLD Tray and rough Growler are having a fight,
Do let us get out of their way;
They snarl, and they growl, and they bark, and they bite!
Oh dear, what a terrible fray!

Why, what foolish fellows! Now, is it not hard
That they can't live together in quiet?
There's plenty of room for them both in the yard,
And I'm sure they have plenty of diet.

But who ever said to old Growler and Tray,
It was naughty to quarrel and fight?
They think it as pretty to fight as to play;
And they do not know wrong from the right.

But when little children, who do know it's wrong,
Are angrily fighting away,
We are sure that to them far more blame must belong,
Than to quarrelsome Growler and Tray.

325

The Honest Ploughman

POOR Tom is a husbandman, healthy and strong,
   He follows his plough as it pushes along,
And trudging behind it he carols a song.

He's up in the morning before the cock crows,
For he should not be idle, he very well knows,
Though some who are idle know that, I suppose.

And when the sun sets, and his work is done soon,
He finds his way home by the light of the moon ·
And she shines in his face, as he whistles a tune.

And when he gets home, (for he never delays),
And sees his neat cot, and the cheerful wood blaze,
His heart glows within him with pleasure and praise.

'Tis those who won't work that mayn't eat, it is said;
But Tom, with good appetite, takes his brown bread,
And then cheerful and happy he goes to his bed.

The Little Beggar Girl

THERE'S a poor beggar going by,
    I see her looking in ;
She's just about as big as I,
    Only so very thin.

She has no shoes upon her feet,
    She is so very poor ;
And hardly anything to eat :
    I pity her, I'm sure.

But I have got nice clothes, you know,
    And meat, and bread, and fire ;
And dear mamma, that loves me so,
    And all that I desire

If I were forced to stroll so far,
    Oh dear, what should I do !
I wish she had a kind mamma,
    Just such a one as you

Here, little girl, come back again,
    And hold that ragged hat,
And I will put a penny in ;
    There, buy some bread with that.

327

Rhymes for the Nursery

Poor Puss

OH, Harry! my dear, do not hurt the poor cat,
    For Pussy, I'm sure, will not thank you for that;
She was doing no harm, as she laid on the mat.

Suppose some great giant, amazingly strong,
Were to kick you, and squeeze you, and drive you
    along ;
Now, would you not think it exceedingly wrong ?

And really, my dear, you're as greatly to blame,
For you're serving poor Pussy exactly the same,
And yet she's so gentle, and quiet, and tame.

She is under the table, quite out of your way,
And why should you tease her, and drive her away ?
She thinks you're in earnest, if you call it play.

There, now go and call her, and stroke her again,
And never, my love, give poor animals pain,
For you know, when you hurt them, they cannot
    complain.

The Little Ants

A LITTLE black ant found a large grain of wheat,
  Too heavy to lift or to roll ;
So he begged of a neighbour he happened to meet,
  To help it down into his hole.

' I've got my own work to see after,' said he ;
  ' You must shift for yourself, if you please ,'
So he crawled off, as selfish and cross as could be,
  And lay down to sleep at his ease.

Just then a black brother was passing the road,
  And seeing his neighbour in want,
Came up and assisted him in with his load ,
  For he was a good-natured ant.

Let all who this story may happen to hear,
  Endeavour to profit by it ;
For often it happens that children appear
  As cross as the ant every bit.

And the good-natured ant, who assisted his brother,
  May teach those who choose to be taught,
That if little insects are kind to each other,
  Then children most certainly ought.

The Meadows

WE'LL go to the meadows, where cowslips do grow,
  And buttercups, looking as yellow as gold ,
And daisies and violets beginning to blow ;
  For it is a most beautiful sight to behold.

The little bee humming about them is seen,
  The butterfly merrily dances along ,
The grasshopper chirps in the hedges so green,
  And the linnet is singing his liveliest song.

The birds and the insects are happy and gay,
  The beasts of the field they are glad and rejoice,
And we will be thankful to GOD every day,
  And praise His great name in a loftier voice.

He made the green meadows, He planted the flowers,
  He sent His bright sun in the heavens to blaze,
He created these wonderful bodies of ours,
  And as long as we live we will sing of His praise.

The Wasp and the Bee

The Wasp and the Bee

A WASP met a Bee that was just buzzing by,
And he said, ' My dear cousin, can you tell me why
You are loved so much better by people than I ?

' Why, my back is as bright and as yellow as gold,
And my shape is most elegant, too, to behold ;
Yet nobody likes me for that, I am told !'

Says the Bee, ' My dear cousin, it's all very true,
But indeed they would love me no better than you,
If I were but half as much mischief to do !

' You have a fine shape, and a delicate wing,
And they own you are handsome, but then there's one thing
Which they cannot put up with, and that is your sting.

' Now I put it at once to your own common sense,
If you are not so ready at taking offence
As to sting them on every trifling pretence ?

' Though my dress is so homely and plain, as you see,
And I have a small sting, they're not angry with me,
Because I'm a busy and good-natured Bee !'

From this pray let ill-natured people beware,
Because I am sure, if they do not take care,
That they'll never be loved, if they're ever so fair.

The Little Girl who was Naughty, and who was afterwards very sorry for it

HERE'S morning again, and a good fireside,
  And such nice bread-and-milk, in a basin quite
    full;
How kindly you always my breakfast provide,
  But something's the matter, mamma, you're so dull!

You don't smile to meet me, nor call me your dear,
  Nor place your arms round me so kind on your knee;
I must have done something that's naughty, I fear,
  For I'm sure you are grieved.—are you angry with me?

Oh! now I remember, last night how I cried,
  And you said that you could not then give me a kiss;
I know that I might have been good if I'd tried·
  But indeed I am grieved I behaved so amiss

To be so ill-temper'd and naughty and rude
  To you, was unkind, and exceedingly wrong,
I'm ashamed when I think of how ill I've behaved;—
  You ought not to kiss me for ever so long.

Yet indeed I do love you, and really will try
  To remember, before I again act amiss,
That you, and that God who's above in the sky,
  Cannot love little girls who're as naughty as this!

The Dunce of a Kitten

COME, pussy, will you learn to read ?
   I've got a pretty book :
Nay, turn this way, you must, indeed :
   Fie, there's a sulky look.

Here is a pretty picture, see,
   An Apple, and great A :
How stupid you will always be,
   If you do nought but play.

Come, A, B, C, an easy task,
   What any one could do :
I will do anything you ask,
   For dearly I love you.

Now how I'm vexed you are so dull,
   You have not learnt it half ;
You'll grow a downright simpleton,
   And make the people laugh.

Mamma told me so, I declare,
   And made me quite ashamed ,
So I resolved no pains to spare,
   Nor like a dunce be blamed.

Well, get along, you naughty kit,
   And after mice go look !
I'm glad that I have got more wit—
   I love my pretty book.

Rhymes for the Nursery

A Very Sorrowful Story

I'LL tell you a story, come, sit on my knee,
A true and a pitiful one it shall be,
About a poor man, and an old man was he.

He'd a fine merry boy (such another as you),
And he did for him all that a father could do,
For he was a kind father as ever I knew

So he hoped that, one day, when his darling should grow
A fine hearty man, he'd remember, you know,
To thank his old father for loving him so.

But what do you think came of all this at last?
Why, after a great many years had gone past,
And the good-natured father grew old very fast,

Instead of remembering how kind he had been,
This boy did not care for his father a pin,
But he bade him begone, for he should not come in

So he wandered about in the frost and the snow!
For he had not a place in the world where to go:
And you'd almost have cried to have heard the wind
    blow.

And the tears, poor old man, oh ! how fast they did pour !
As he shivered with cold at his wicked child's door.
Did you ever, now, hear such a story before ?

APPENDICES

Appendix I

Poems omitted from the Final Editions of
'Original Poems' and 'Rhymes
for the Nursery'

FROM 'ORIGINAL POEMS'

Nimble Dick

M Y boy, be cool, do things by rule,
    And then you'll do them right ·
A story true I'll tell to you,
    'Tis of a luckless wight.

He'd never wait, was ever late,
    Because he was so quick.
This shatter-brain did thus obtain
    The name of Nimble Dick.

All in his best young Dick was drest,
    Cries he, ' I'm very dry !'
Tho' glass, and jug, and china mug,
    On sideboard stood hard by

With skip and jump unto the pump,
    With open'd mouth he goes :
The water out ran from the spout,
    And wetted all his clothes,

337

A fine tureen, as e'er was seen,
  On dinner table stood ;
Says John, ' 'Tis hot,'—says Dick, ' 'Tis not—
  I know the soup is good.'

His brother bawl'd, ' Yourself you'll scald—
  O Dick, you're so uncouth !'
Dick fill'd his spoon, and then as soon
  Convey'd it to his mouth.

And soon about he spurts it out,
  And cries, ' O wicked soup !'
His mother chid, his father bid
  Him from the table troop

All in dispatch, he made a match
  To run a race with Bill ;
' My boy,' said he, ' I'll win, you'll see ;
  I'll beat you, that I will '

With merry heart, now off they start,
  Like poneys in full speed ;
Soon Bill he pass'd, for very fast
  This Dicky ran indeed

But hurry all, Dick got a fall,
  And whilst he sprawling lay,
Bill reach'd the post, and Dicky lost,
  And Billy won the day.

' Bring here my pad,' now cries the lad
  Unto the servant John ;
' I'll mount astride, this day I'll ride,
  So put the saddle on.'

No time to waste, 'twas brought in haste,
  Dick long'd to have it back'd .
With spur and boot on leg and foot,
  His whip he loudly crack'd.

The Mother's Wish

The mane he grasp'd, the crupper clasp'd,
　　And leap'd up from the ground ;
All smart and spruce—the girt was loose,
　　He turn'd the saddle round.

Then down he came, the scoff and shame
　　Of all the standers by ·
Poor Dick, alack ! upon his back,
　　Beneath the horse did lie.

Still slow and sure success secure,
　　And be not over quick ;
For method's sake, a warning take
　　From hasty Nimble Dick.

The Mother's Wish

MAY cloudless beams of grace and truth
　　Adorn my daughter's op'ning youth !
Long, happy in her native home,
Among its fragrant groves to roam.
May choicest blessings her attend,
Blest in her parents, sisters, friend !
May no rude wish assail her breast,
To love this world, by all confest
As only giv'n us to prepare
For one eternal, bright and fair.
This world shall then no force retain,
Its siren voice shall charm in vain ;
Religion's aid true peace will bring,
Her voice with joy shall praises sing,
To Him whose streams of mercy flow,
To cheer the heart o'ercharged with woe ,
And whilst retirement's sweets we prove,
For ever praise redeeming love.

Written at Barming

To Maria

HOW happy the days of your youth,
  Instructed in virtue and truth,
By the parents you love and revere,
Your dwelling is healthy and neat,
Of sisters so dear the retreat,
And of neighbours abundance are near

Oh, think whence these blessings arise,
From a Being so gracious and wise,
And should they by Him be withdrawn ;
Should ev'ry degree of distress,
My dearest of daughters oppress
When torn from the sweet verdant lawn :

From what must she then seek relief,
When her mind is disturbèd with grief,
But from GOD, who but chastens to bless ?
Fine garments, rich food, and bright wine,
With which the voluptuous dine,
Enervate beyond all redress.

In the sad sober moments of woe,
Which each mortal is destin'd to know,
With joy will a Christian perceive,
That life as a vision recedes,
That faith, render'd bright by good deeds,
A blessèd reward will receive.

Should you as a mother or wife,
Be call'd on to act in this life,
Oh ! strive ev'ry virtue to trace ;
On the minds you may have to attend,
Join at once the kind mother and friend,
And pray for their virtue and grace.

Written at Barming

340

The Poor Little Baby

FROM 'RHYMES FOR THE NURSERY'

The Poor Little Baby

DOWN, down, in the pit-hole poor baby is gone,
The cold earth did rattle its coffin upon,
And there they have left it for ever to keep,
And a little green hillock shows where it doth sleep.

Poor baby ! I saw it beginning to play,
And smile at mamma, in her lap as it lay,
And hold out its little hands joyfully, thus,
To go to her arms when she took it from nurse.

But its little hands never will move any more,
And it never will smile, as it usèd before,
For it panted, and struggled, and drew a hard breath,
And then it lay still—and they callèd it death !

Ah, dear little baby, it was a sad sight,
Its eyes they were shut, and its face it was white ;
I went up to kiss it, and bid it good-bye,
And its cheeks felt so cold, I was ready to cry !

Now down in the pit-hole it resteth its head,
With only the earth, that's so cold for its bed ;
And let me remember, that I too shall die,
And then in the pit-hole I also must lie.

Charles and Animals

THE cow has a horn, and the fish has a gill;
  The horse has a hoof, and the duck has a bill;
The bird has a wing, that on high he may sail;
And the lion a mane, and the monkey a tail;
And they swim, or they fly, or they walk, or they
    eat,
With fin, or with wing, or with bill, or with feet.

And Charles has two hands, with five fingers to each,
On purpose to work with, to hold and to reach;
No birds, beasts, or fishes, for work or for play,
Have any thing half so convenient as they;
But if he don't use them, and *keep* them in use,
He'd better have had but two legs, like a goose.

JANE.

One Little Boy[*]

I'M a little gentleman,
  And exceeding smart I am,
Very handsome clothes I wear,
And I live on dainty fare,
And whenever out I ride,
I've a servant by my side.

And I never, all the day,
Need do any thing but play,
Nor even soil my little hand,
Because I am so very grand,
O! I'm very glad, I'm sure,
I need not labour, like the poor.

* See page 286 for the contrast —ED

The Undutiful Boy

For I think I could not bear,
Such old shabby clothes to wear,
To lie upon so hard a bed,
And only live on barley bread ,
And what is worse, too, every day
To have to work as hard as they.

The Undutiful Boy

LITTLE Harry, come along,
    And mamma will sing a song,
All about a naughty lad,
Tho' a mother kind he had.

He never minded what she said,
But only laughed at her instead ;
And then did just the same, I've heard,
As if she had not said a word.

He would not learn to read his book,
But wisdom's pleasant way forsook ;
In wicked boys he took delight,
And learnt to quarrel and to fight.

And when he saw his mother cry,
And heard her heave a bitter sigh,
To think she'd such a wicked son,
He never car'd for what he'd done !

I hope my little Harry will
Mind all I say, and love me still ;
For 'tis his mother's greatest joy,
To think he's not a wicked boy.

The Great Lord

A VERY great lord lives near Thomas's cot,
Who servants, and coaches, and horses, has got ;
And yet his poor neighbour, Tom, envies him not.

For coaches, and horses, and delicate food,
Can't make people happy unless they are good ;
But then he is idle, and wicked, and rude.

He never does any thing all the day long,
Altho' he is able, and healthy, and strong :
He does nothing right, but he often does wrong.

And then he's as vain as he ever can be,
He wears gaudy clothes, that poor people may see ;
And laughs at good folks, that are better than he.

And tho' he's so rich, and so great, and so high,
He does no more good than a worm or a fly ;
And no one would miss him, if he were to die.

I think 'tis much better, for all that I see,
A poor honest ploughman, like Thomas, to be,
Than a fine wealthy lord, but as useless as he.

344

Second Thoughts are Best

I HATE being scolded, and having a rout,
  I've a good mind to stand in the corner and pout ;
And if mamma calls me, I will not come out.

Yes, yes, here I'll keep, I'm resolv'd on it quite,
With my face to the wall, and my back to the light,
And I'll not speak a word, if I stand here all night.

And yet mamma says, when I'm naughty and cry,
She scolds me to make me grow good by and by
And that, all the time, she's as sorry as I.

And she says, when I'm naughty and will not obey,
If she were to let me go on in that way,
I should grow up exceedingly wicked one day.

O then, what a very sad girl I should be,
To be sulky because she was angry with me,
And grieve such a very kind mother as she !

Well, then, I'll go to her directly and say,
Forgive me this once, my dear mother, I pray ;
For that will be better than sulking all day.

Appendix II

THE WEDDING AMONG THE FLOWERS

BY

ANN TAYLOR

The Wedding among the Flowers

IN a grand convocation which Flora enacted,
   Where the bus'ness of all her domain was trans-
     acted,
'Twas hinted, there yet remain'd one regulation
To perfect her glorious administration.
To some, strength and masculine beauty were giv'n,
Majestical air, and an eye meeting heav'n ;
Hidden virtues to many, to others perfume,
Through each variation of sweetness and bloom :
'Twas therefore suggested, with Flora's compliance,
To unite ev'ry charm in some splendid alliance.
   The royal assent to the motion was gain'd,
'Twas pass'd at three sittings, and duly ordain'd.
   'Twas now most amusing to traverse the shade,
And hear the remarks that were privately made
Such whispers, enquiries, and investigations !
Such balancing merits, and marshalling stations.
The nobles protested they never would yield
To debase their high sap with the weeds of the field ;

The Wedding among the Flowers

For, indeed, there was nothing so vulgar and rude,
As to let ev'ry ill-bred young wild flow'r intrude .
Their daughters should never dishonour their houses,
By taking such rabble as these for their spouses!
  At length, my Lord SUNFLOWER, whom public opinion
Confess'd as the pride of the blooming dominion,
Avow'd an affection he'd often betray'd,
For sweet Lady LILY, the queen of the shade ;
And said, should her friends nor the public withstand,
He would dare to solicit her elegant hand.
  A whisper, like that which on fine summer eves
Young zephyrs address to the frolicsome leaves,
Immediately ran through the whole congregation,
Expressive of pleasure, and high approbation.
No line was degraded, no family pride
Insulted, by either the bridegroom or bride ;
For in him all was majesty, beauty, and splendor,
In her all was elegant, simple, and tender.
  Now nothing remain'd but to win her consent,
And Miss IRIS, her friend, as the messenger went,
The arts of entreaty and argument trying,
Till at length she return'd, and announc'd her com-
    plying.
Complete satisfaction the tidings convey'd,
And whispers and smiles dimpled over the shade.
The COCKSCOMB, indeed, and a few POWDER'D BEAUX,
Who were not little vain of their figure and clothes,
Look'd down with chagrin which they could not dis-
    guise,
That *they* were not fix'd on to carry the prize.
At length the young nobleman ventur'd to name
The following spring, and supported his claim,
By duly consulting a reverend seer,
DANDELION, who augur'd the wedding that year,
Mov'd to give his opinion by breath of perfume,
And nodding assent with his silvery plume.

The Wedding among the Flowers

For licence, his lordship in person applied
To the high CROWN IMPERIAL, whose court he descried
By the GOLDEN ROD, ensign of state, by his side:
Returning from thence in the course of his journey,
He order'd the deeds of JONQUIL, the attorney;
And, anxious a speedy conclusion to bring,
Set LOVECHAIN and GOLD-DUST to work on the ring.

   Now April was dimpled with smiles, and the day
Was fix'd for the first of luxuriant May:
Along the parterre, in the shade or the sun,
All was bus'ness, and bustle, and frolic, and fun;
For, as Flora had granted a full dispensation
To ev'ry gay tribe in her blooming creation,
By which at the festival all might appear,
Who else were on duty but parts of the year,
There was now such a concourse of beauty and grace,
As had not, since Eden, appear'd in one place;
And cards were dispers'd, with consent of the fair,
To ev'ry great family through the parterre.

   There was one city lady, indeed, that the bride
Did not wish to attend, which was Miss LONDON
    PRIDE,
And his lordship declar'd he would rather not meet
So doubtful a person as young BITTER SWEET.
Sir MICHAELMAS DAISY was ask'd to appear,
But was gone out of town for best part of the year:
And though he was sent for, NARCISSUS declin'd
Out of pique, and preferr'd to keep sulking behind;
For, having beheld his fine form in the water,
He thought himself equal to any flow'r's daughter;
And would not consent to increase a parade,
The hero of which, he himself should have made.
Dr CAMOMILE was to have been of the party,
But was summon'd to town, to old Alderman Hearty.
Old ALOE, a worthy, respectable don,
Could not go in the clothes that just then he had on,

The Wedding among the Flowers

And his taylor was such a slow fellow, he guess'd
That it might be a cent'ry before he was dress'd.
Excuses were sent, too, from very near all
The ladies residing at Great GREEN HOUSE HALL,
Who had been so confin'd, were so chilly and spare,
It might cost them their lives to be out in the air.
The SENSITIVE PLANT hop'd her friends would excuse her,
It thrill'd ev'ry nerve in her frame to refuse her,
But she did not believe she had courage to view
The solemn transaction she'd summon'd her to.
WIDOW WAIL had a ticket, but would not attend,
For fear her low spirits should sadden her friend ·
And, too wild to regard either lady or lord,
HONEY-SUCKLE, as usual, was gadding abroad.
Notwithstanding all which, preparations were made,
In the very first style, for the splendid parade.
    One CLOTH-PLANT, a clothier of settled repute,
Undertook to provide ev'ry beau with a suit,
Trimm'd with BACHELOR'S BUTTONS, but these, I presume,
Were rejected, as out of the proper costume.
Miss SATIN FLOW'R, fancy-dress maker from town,
Had silks of all colours and patterns come down ;
And long LADIES' RIBBON could hardly prepare
Her trimmings so fast as bespoke by the fair.
Two noted perfumers, from Shrubbery Lane,
Messrs MUSK-ROSE and LAVENDER, essenc'd the train ,
And ere the damp weather of April expir'd,
The whole blooming band was completely attir'd.
    At length the bright morning, with glittering eye,
Peep'd o'er the green earth from the rose-colour'd sky ;
And soon as the lark flitted out of her nest,
The bridal assembly was merry and drest.
Among the most lovely, far lovelier shone
The bride, with an elegance purely her own :
Her tall, slender figure green tissue array'd,
With di'monds strung loose on the shining brocade :

349

The Wedding among the Flowers

A cap of white velvet, in graceful costume
Adorn'd her fair forehead—a silvery plume,
Tipp'd with gold, from the centre half negligent hung,
With strings of white pearl scatter'd loosely among.
The last, (such as fairies are fancied to wear,)
Aurora herself had dispos'd in her hair.
To meet her, and welcome the high-omen'd day,
The bridgroom stepp'd forth in majestic array.
A rough velvet suit, mingled russet and green,
Around his fine figure, broad flowing, was seen ,
His front, warm and manly, a diadem grac'd,
Of regal appearance, resplendent as chaste ·
The centre was pucker'd in velvet of brown,
With golden vandykes, which encircled the crown.
Since Nature's first morning, ne'er glitter'd a pair,
The one so commanding, the other so fair !
Many ladies of fashion had offer'd to wait
As bridemaid, the honour was reckon'd so great :
These fam'd for their beauty, for fragrancy those,
ANEMONE splendid, or sweet-smelling ROSE ;
But, gentle and free from a tincture of pride,
A sweet country cousin was call'd by the bride,
Who long in a VALLEY had shelter'd unknown,
Or trac'd to the shade by her sweetness alone.
She, timid appear'd in the meekest array,
Like pearls of clear dew on an evergreen spray.
Now mov'd the procession from dressing-room bow'rs,
A brilliant display of illustrious flow'rs ;
Young HEART'S-EASE in purple and gold ran before,
To welcome them in at the great temple door,
Where old Bishop MONK'S-HOOD had taken his stand,
To weave and to sanction the conjugal band :
The TRUMPETER-SUCKLING, with musical air,
Preceded as herald, and then the young pair ,
With little Miss LILY, as bridemaid, behind
Alone, her fair head on her bosom reclin'd,

The Wedding among the Flowers

The old Duke of Piony, richly array'd
In coquelicot, headed the long cavalcade ;
Duchess Dowager Rose leading up at his side,
With her daughters, some blooming, some fair as the bride.
My lady Carnation, excessively dashing,
Roug'd highly, and new in the Rotterdam fashion,
Discoursing of rank and of pedigree came,
With a beau of distinction, Van Tulip by name.
Field-officer Poppy, in trim *militaire*,
An unfortunate youth, Hyacinthus the fair ,
With Major Convolvulus, fresh from parade,
And his son, though a Minor, in purple cockade.
A pair from the country, affecting no show,
Pretty Betsy the belle, and Sweet William the beau,
Succeeded ,—and next. in the simplest attire,
Miss Jessamine pale, and her lover Sweet Briar.
Auricula came in puce velvet and white,
With her spouse Polyanthus, a rich city knight ·
Messrs. Stocks, from 'Change Alley, in crimson array,
The twin-brother Larkspurs, two fops of the day ,
With light-hearted Columbine, playing the fool,
And footing away like a frolic from school.
Then a distant relation, 'twas said, of the bride,
Water Lily, a nymph from the rivulet's side ·
And last, hand in hand at the end of the train,
Violetta and Daisy, from Hazelnut Lane.

Mezereon had fully design'd to be there,
But was only half drest, and oblig'd to forbear ;
And the Evening Primrose was pale with chagrin.
That her cap did not come till the day had clos'd in :
So each remain'd pouting behind in the shade,
As winding along mov'd the brilliant parade.

At length, the fair temple appear'd to the view,
All blushing with beauty, and spangled with dew
Tall Hollyhock pillars encircled it round,
With tendrils of Pea and sweet Eglantine bound

351

The Wedding among the Flowers

The roof was a trellis of myrtle and vine,
Which knots and festoons of Nasturtium combine,
Surmounting each pillar, the cornice display'd
The Midsummer Starwort, relieving the shade;
And, wreath'd into loops of the tenderest green,
Antirrhinum wav'd loose to the zephyrs between.
The Passion-flow'r fond, to the portico clung,
And Guelder-rose glitter'd the foliage among:
A mossy mosaic the pavement display'd,
With tufts of Hepatica richly inlaid,
And high in the centre an altar was rear'd,
Which wreathen with net-work of flowers appear'd;
Where a sunbeam each herb aromatic consum'd,
Condens'd by clear dew-drops the dome that illum'd:
Above were suspended the merry BLUE BELLS,
Holy rite to enliven with musical swells.

And now the train enters, the altar burns bright,
Sweet odours escape from the centrical light;
Before the green shrine, the young couple await
Each form ceremonious ordain'd by the state,
And mystical rite, understood but by flow'rs,
Which elude observation of eyes such as ours:
'Twas only perceiv'd, that the Bishop profound
Clear dews from his urn sprinkled thrice on the
    ground;
And zephyr, or some such invisible thing,
Thrice flutter'd the air with his butterfly wing.
At length the rite clos'd in a grand benediction,
And merriment burst without any restriction.

Now blush'd in the banquet, along the parterre,
Each dainty, that nature or art could prepare.
DAMASK ROSE on the lawn had a tablecloth spread,
The FLESH PLANT provided the dish at the head,
And CORNBOTTLE furnish'd the table with bread
Housewife BUTTERCUP sent a supply from her churn;
The SNOWDROP ic'd dews in a white crocus urn;

The Wedding among the Flowers

And CANDY TUFT, skill'd in the arts of preserving,
A splendid dessert had the honour of serving
ROSE BURGUNDY, Vintner, the goblet supplied
With neat foreign wines, and made COWSLIP beside;
Campanula cups, fill'd with gentle spring rain,
Were serv'd to the ladies who wish'd for it plain.
And all was so elegant, splendid, and rare,
That I could not name half the fine things that were there;
When finish'd, SNAPDRAGONS produc'd a good joke,
And ROCKETS went up to amuse the young folk.
  In return for past favours, a band of young bees
Humm'd a sweet mellow air through the neighbouring
    trees;
And Linnet and Lark, as by accident, met
And surpris'd the young pair with a charming duet.
  And now mirth and revelry were at their height,
The little ones crept to the shade in affright,
The ladies had danc'd in the heat of the sun,
Till their dresses were limp, and their spirits outdone;
And Flora, who witness'd the scene with concern,
Beckon'd forward to Vesper, to empty her urn.
At once, as by magic, the merriment died;
Not a whisper was heard, not a gambol was tried!
Return'd to their stations, in border or bed,
Each shut up his eye, or hung graceful her head;
And those who had left foreign mountains and vales,
Rode home, in snug parties, on zephyrs and gales;
So that ere the first star ventur'd out with a beam,
They were all sound asleep, and beginning to dream!

A.

Appendix III

Five Pieces from Adelaide O'Keeffe's
'Original Poems Calculated to Improve
the Mind of Youth and Allure
it to Virtue.' 1808

The Poney

MY poney can amble, my poney can trot,
    My poney can gallop so swift—
My poney looks pleased on his back when I've got,
    Up some one must give me a lift.

I gracefully sit in my saddle with ease,
    To manage my poney with art ;
My toes I hold in, and I keep tight my knees :
    I have my whole lesson by heart.

I low hold my bridle, and steady and still,
    Nor wriggle, nor sidle about ;
I lean myself forward, when going up hill,
    And down hill, lean backward, no doubt

I let my curb bridle be loose on his neck,
    Except he gets running away ,
I then take it up, and his spirit I check ;
    Again comes the snaffle in play.

The Poney

I pity my poney, my poney I love ;
   The whip I but sparingly use ;
At shake of my bridle he onward will move ;
   Why should I my power abuse ?

Or wantonly dig his poor flank with my spur,
   Or mangle his sides with my whip ?
Such cruelty casts on that horseman a slur,
   Who merits a jade and a rip.

Tho' now I'm a boy, yet when I'm grown big,
   I never will canter thro' towns,
My neck may be broke, if I'm cross'd by a pig,
   I'll gallop o'er commons and downs.

Whenever my poney attempts to be shy,
   And starts at a stone or a bush,
I make him turn back, put his nose to it nigh,
   Then fear he'll not value a rush.

My poney's a toper, he'd fain stop to drink
   At every pond he comes to,
He's only a poney ; for him I must think ;
   No, no, my good friend, this won't do.

A drink you may take, when we're near our next
   stage ,
   Dear horse, of your health I take care—
And for your obedience my word I engage,
   A pottle of oats is your fare.

The ostler sha'nt from you one grain take away ,
   He'll call me a troublesome fool ·
But whilst you're at dinner with you I will stay,
   Altho' my own dinner should cool.

The Kite

MY Kite is three feet broad, and six feet long;
　　The standard straight, the bender tough and
　　　　strong,
And to its milk-white breast five painted stars belong.

Grand and majestic soars my paper kite,
Thro' trackless skies it takes its lofty flight
Nor lark nor eagle flies to such a noble height.

As in the field I stand and hold the twine,
Swift I unwind, to give it length of line,
Yet swifter it ascends, nor will to earth incline.

Like a small speck, so high I see it sail,
I hear its pinions flutter in the gale,
And, like a flock of wild geese, sweeps its flowing tail.

Tom at Dinner

ONE day little Tom in his clean pin-afore,
　　Was seated at table, and dinner served in;
Tho' Tom was not helped, yet with patience he bore
　Whilst every one round him was wagging a chin.

They laughed, eat, and drank, with a hearty good cheer,
　The hot smoaking dishes looked tempting and nice;
Still Tom was forgot, tho' his hunger severe
　Now wanted no dainties his wish to entice.

At length, to his father, with voice soft and sweet,
　'I'll thank you,' said he, 'for some salt, if you please.'
'Some salt!'—'Yes,' said Tom, 'when you give me
　　some meat,
　'My salt I'll have ready—I don't wish to teaze.'

356

Jack at Dinner

All present was struck with his patience and wit,
  His mother caressed him with kisses so kind,
His father then gave him the choicest tit-bit
  Thus Tommy got praises and jovially dined.

Jack at Dinner

JACK was rugged, Jack was tough,
  Jack no manners had ;
Jack unpolished was and rough,
  No one liked the lad

Jack was by his mother brought
  To a splendid feast,
Being better fed than taught,
  What an awkward guest !

Jack would pick a mutton bone,
  Held with both his hands ;
When he saw his mother frown,
  He'd obey commands.

From the bone one hand he took,
  One hand held it still ,
Still 'twas wrong, he in her look,
  Read his mother's will.

That hand then he took away,
  What a sight uncouth !
In his teeth the bone did stay,
  All across his mouth.

Every eye with wonder turned
  On young Jack's broad face ,
Mother's cheeks with blushes burned,
  For her son's disgrace.

357

Poems from Adelaide

From good manners some are mute,
  Pitying her pain ;
Some now whisper, ' What a brute !'
  Some laugh out amain

Laughing, till their eyes run o'er,
  At the ill-bred toad,
Mother says that never more,
  Jack shall dine abroad

Little Fanny Negative

WHO says that I ever once frowned ?
  Who says that my answers are simple ?
Who says that my cheek isn't round ?
  Who says that my chin wants a dimple ?

Who says in warm water I wash
  My face, or my neck, or my hands ?
Who says I am hasty and rash,
  Or sulky when mother commands ?

Who says that I listen at door ?
  Who says, through a key-hole I peep ?
Who says, I've been harsh to the poor ?
  Or found after sunrise asleep ?

Who says that I creep like a snail,
  Whenever on business I go ?
Who says, I sit picking my nail,
  Whenever I've something to do ?

Who says, I can't finish my task ?
  Who says, though of money I'm scant,
That meanly a present I'd ask
  Of granny, or uncle, or aunt ?

Never Delay

Who says, when I've any thing good,
  I ever refuse to give share?
Who says that I'm forward or rude,
  Or romp like a kid or a bear?

Who says that I hop as I walk?
  Who says that I jump down the stairs?
Who says that in sermon I talk,
  Or wickedly mutter my prayers?

Who says, though I should do amiss,
  I'd seek by a lie to get free?
Whoe'er says a word of all this,
  I'm sure knows but little of me.

―――――

Fifteen Pieces from Adelaide O'Keeffe's 'Poems for Young Children.' 1849

Never Delay

THE SCHOOL BOYS

'TIS holiday time, so hurra for the fair,
    The fair that is held on the Green,
Come, Thomas, have done with your slates and
    forbear,
  And bravely enjoy the gay scene

'There are round-a-bouts, booths, and such fine
    painted things,
  And gingerbread nuts by the dozen,
And large caravans, with wild beasts, and such
    things!
  So come along, Tom, my grave cousin '―

Poems from Adelaide

'Stop, stop, my good fellow!' his cousin replies,
  'Remember our holiday task,
Not a line have you written, tho' looking so wise.
  Now where is your theme, let me ask?

'To-morrow, you know, we must go back to
    school;
  There! mine it is finished—I'm free
To see the wild beasts without playing the fool,
  Tho' fairs are not pleasant to me.'—

The morrow it came, and to school they both went,
  The master he called them by name,
Tom modestly smiling quick up to him went,
  But Edward stood covered with shame.

'Well done, Master Thomas,' the schoolmaster
    said,
  'Your exercise claims all my praise,
But for Edward the idler, I very much dread,
  He'll suffer confinement some days.

'So you, Master Neddy, with looks cross and glum,
  Stay within, and your exercise write,
Whilst Tom joins his schoolfellows—come, Thomas,
    come!
  To cricket!—Oh, Tom, what delight!'

Temperance

DAN AND HIS CHERRY PIE

FAIR Susan was a temperate child,
    And cared not for nice fare,
But Daniel pastry loved, and wild
    He was for dainties rare.

On cherry tart this day they dined,
    That is, young Susan did,
But nurse no where could Daniel find,
    She thought he must have hid.

But no, a-scampering he would run,
    With other boys to Blackfriais' road,
To make nurse seek him—Oh, what fun!
    A thought of home was not bestowed.

Full late returned—he asked to dine,
    Insisted on his cherry pie.
'What! cherry pie at night!—'tis nine,'
    Said Nurse—'Oh no, sir; fie, oh fie!'

'Give me my pie, and hold your prate.'
    'Upon my word, sir, pretty talk;
Eat it, and see what soon your state.'
    'My appetite you shall not balk.'

'Then take it—but at least take care
    You swallow not the stones.'—
'I'll swallow what I please—beware
    My anger—they'll break no bones.'

Poems from Adelaide

Dan ate his pie, he ate it all,
  Both cherries, stones, and paste ,
Then ask'd for ale¹ with lordly call,
  But nurse forbade in haste.

' I wish your parents were returned,
  You would not dare act thus,
But, sir, they'll both be much concern'd.'—
  ' Dear nurse, don't make a fuss.'

' Your sister dined at two o'clock,
  And sparingly she ate,
But you at night lay in a stock,
  And eat and cram at such a rate,

' That you'll be ill, I do expect,
  And never join the children's ball.
Now go to bed, and pray reflect,
  You are not six feet tall.'

Dan went to bed—oh, sad to say ¹
He stayed in bed the whole next day,
And when the joyful ball-night came.
He hid himself with pain and shame.

With sickly feel and aching head,
He crept up slowly to his bed,
Whilst Susan joined the merry dance ;
Such are the fruits of TEMPERANCE.

Johnny flinging Stones

' I 'M kill'd! I'm dead! I'll surely die,
Papa, come here—I really fear
That I must die, and presently!'

Thus Johnny roar'd,
A little coward!
His face all over blood,
His clothes all drench'd in mud.

Papa drew near, at first in fear,
But soon he could decide
That Master John had mischief done,
Which cannot be denied.

' How came your face in that *red* case?
Come, Johnny, tell the truth,
You're not a lying youth '
' Papa, a stone thus smashed my cheek.'
' *Who* flung it, boy?—speak, frankly speak.'

' I threw it my own self at that old man
When after him I ran,
But it struck against a tree
And rebounded full on me ,
And, whilst he harmless stood,
I tumbled in the mud!'

'And truly glad I am,' Papa then said,
'That thus the stone rebounded on *your* head .
May every stone that you in mischief fling
Its own just punishment upon you bring!

'But the truth you have spoken,
My word's never broken, .
So go wash your. face,
Without further disgrace.'

363

Falsehood is Cowardly

FOUR SCHOOL BOYS—A TRUE STORY

' WHO complains that their dinner is bad ?'
    Said the schoolmaster, gruffly and grim ;
' Quickly point out the insolent lad,
    That my anger may fall upon *him*.'

' I never complained '—' No, nor I,'
    Said Dick and Job, Philip and Ned,
Adam, Walter, and Joseph so sly,
    ' Tho' you cane us, sir, 'till we are dead.'

Now this was most *false !*—for they all,
    Had angrily turned from their food,
They were all in one mind, great and small,
    And in truth much was bad—little good.

Then up started Edmund with pride,
    ' 'Twas I, sir !—the truth I'll maintain,
I care not on what you decide,
    Cruel menaces I can disdain.

' Our bread, oh, how musty !—our meat is as bad,
    With hunger we're ready to sink,
We're fatherless boys, and our case is most sad !
    E'en the water we scarcely can drink !'

The master, half pleased, said, ' If such be the truth,
    These *cowards* remain here behind,
Whilst *you* dine with me, my fine-spirited youth,
    Who nobly can thus speak his mind.'   •

364

Truth is Brave

'Oh, no, sir,' the good boy then quickly replied,
   ' With my schoolfellows still let me dine ;
But, sir, see to our food !—for it can't be denied,
   To cheat you some persons combine !'

    .   .   .   .   .

This good advice the master did *not* take,—
   If boys drop off—a school must fail !
When men—they clubbed their money for his sake,
   Or else their master must have died in jail !

Truth is Brave

RICH SCHOOL BOYS—ALSO A TRUE STORY

THESE boys had a play-ground of spacious extent
   To themselves, where they play'd in high glee,
At cricket, bold leap-frog, prison-bars, and swift race,
   And in climbing a noble elm-tree.—

Forbidden all violent pastimes in-doors,
   To their ground was confined all their play,
These orders were never disputed, until
   One very unfortunate day !

A large chandelier, with drop-lustres so fine,
   Had hung o'er the drawing-room table,
All scatter'd and broken, the VICAR this found !
   To account for such ruin who's able ?

That some of his pupils had enter'd, he saw
   By their foot-prints in clay on the floor,
And sadly the curtains of muslin were torn !
   See finger-marks on the glass door !—

Poems from Adelaide

No canings, no floggings, no faggings allowed :
    Each pupil, so well bred, he loved as his son ,
But still there was punishment—·by his own laws,
    And thus their affection and fear he had won.

This chastisement sad was confinement most strict,
    In solitude total within their own room,
' I shrink,' said the Master, 'from punishing *all*,
    Yet never was known once to alter my doom.'

The boys stood abash'd, for not one tried to speak,
    Not one raised his eyes from the floor,
Three days was the sentence the Vicar decreed,
    The boys then cried out, ' We deserve many more !'

Lord SIDNEY (a duke's son) came forward and said,
    With grief and with tears most sincere,
' Oh, pardon them all, sir, the trespass was mine,
    Oh, pardon, them, master most dear !

' A hawk we pursued—and their leader was I,
    Then on *me* let the punishment fall,
We're ten, and *ten* days, strict confinement I'll bear,
    But pardon my schoolfellows all !'

The terms accepted were—Lord Sidney in his room
        A prisoner stay'd :
        But no one play'd
    Until the time was ended of his doom.

      *   *   *   *   *

A few years pass'd away—and Sidney, now a duke,
    Call'd on his master—and *him* his chaplain made :
To give him wealth and power he pleasure took,
    In BISHOP's robes and lawn he's now array'd !

Wilful Richard

THE AUTHOR'S MORAL

Instructors wise, indeed of every kind,
Should sometimes bear this solid truth in mind:
Tho' little boys and girls they govern *now*,
Yet men and women these contrive to grow.

Harsh and kind treatment's all remember'd well,
And many a sad or happy story most could tell,
Ere of their youthful TEENS they bid farewell.

Wilful Richard

' DEAR Aunt, I've had no dinner yet,
          I think the servants all forget
On me in proper time to wait,—
I'm very hungry—and 'tis late.'

' Where have you, Richard, been ?—pray say-
Truly you have been long away;
Employ'd, or idle, *you* best know,
As still alone you choose to go:
The servants certainly *do* talk,
You on the COMMON love to walk.'

' And surely there's no harm in that !'
Cried Dick as sullenly he sat.
' I stayed out long, the day was fine,
And is't for that I'm not to dine ?
'Tis good roast mutton, I was told,
I'm sure it now will all be cold '

' Nor hot, nor cold, you mutton get,
Whether you scold, or beg, or fret,'
His Aunt said, frowning on the lad.
' Your conduct, Richard's very bad,
From mischief you will never keep.
Who has been worrying harmless sheep ?

367

Poems from Adelaide

' Not suffering them to feed in quiet,
But stirring up a perfect riot ;
And can *you* mutton e'er enjoy ?
Mutton *was* sheep, you know, bad boy !
You may have broken their poor bones
By pelting them with heavy stones '

' *You've* dined—and hunger do not feel,
So I'll carve beef, or lamb, or veal,
Poultry, or fish, I do not care,
I am not dainty as to fare,'
Said the spoilt urchin with a frown,
But soon was impudence put down.
His angry uncle now drew near,
And HIM Dick ever held in fear.—

' Go to your room, you wicked boy,
Who loves to hurt, and all destroy !
On sheep, cows, hens, ducks, birds, and chicks
You've played most wanton, cruel tricks.
Milk, cheese, eggs, butter—any meat,
I'll take good care you shall not eat
For many days to come—so *carve*
This good dry bread—or else you starve.'

Dick ate the bread—and water drank,—
He some days after wished to thank
His uncle for this lesson kind,
And promised faithfully to mind
What he had said—and to life's end
Be to all animals a most tender friend.

  *   *   *   *   *

His word he kept—a man now grown,
A better heart was never known.

The Window-Pane at Night

'OH, what is the matter, my child!
  Your looks are most awfully wild,—
    Why leave off your usual play?
Not noisy, for I heard not a sound,—
Now you throw down your doll on the ground,—
    Do listen, my Maud, and obey.

' Here's plenty of light—as you see,
Tho' you played in the dark, far from me,—
    Behind the red curtains you ran,
But now you rush frightened about,
Of the reason you leave me in doubt,
    Pray tell me the cause—if you can.'

' Papa, at the window I saw !'——
' An owl, I suppose, or jackdaw.'
    ' Oh no, but a robber, I'm sure !
She stared at me full in the face !'
' What, one of the poor gipsy race ?'—
    ' Why, no, I can't say she looked *poor*.

' Her face is as rosy as mine;
Her eyes are bright blue—and they shine—
    But yet she began to look pale,
And open'd her mouth as if crying,
I felt as if *I*, too, was dying !'
    ' Well, this is a wondrous tale !'

' O cruel papa ! how you laugh !
As if 'twere a cow or a calf,
    That really *is* your belief.
Papa might I think believe *me*—
Do go to the window and see,
    Then send out and catch the young thief'

He took little Maud in his arms,
And said, 'These are foolish alarms,
   The pretty "*young thief*" I have caught !
Come now to the window with me,
And then you will speedily see
   The wonder the window-glass wrought.'

Quickly holding her up to a pane,
She saw the same face come again !
   And there was papa's face also !
Convinced now, she bashfully smiled,
The glass show'd a sweet smiling child !
     ' Then this is the case,
     I saw my own face ! '
   Which truth little Maud was most happy
   to know.

Harry, the Arrogant Boy, and Sambo

' QUICK, brush my clothes, and clean my boots,
   I'm going on the water ;
To row a boat my humour suits,
   I'll learn my lessons after !'

' Supposing master *now* sit down,
   And first his lessons learn ?'
' How free you speak, you saucy clown !'
   Said Harry, loud and stern.

' I'd have you know, my slave you are,
   Ay, slave ! you need not stare—
You're black, I'm white, and better far !—
   To mutter do not dare.

Harry, the Arrogant Boy

'But clean my boots, and brush my clothes,
　As I said once before!—
And not *that* suit—I'm tired of those,
　Which yesterday I wore'

' Why, SAMBO! you are deaf, I think,
　Or will you not obey?
You surly look—your eyes you wink!
　I'm losing all the day'

' Then you will not, I see, comply
　With my most just commands?
Must I myself brush boots!—what! I!
　With these soft, pretty hands!'—

In silence Sambo cleaned his knives,
　While Harry kick'd his boots,—
And soon the slender boat arrives,
　With boys in rowing suits!

'Come, Harry, come! are you not ready?
　With you we number eight.
To row to Chelsea,—Ho, boys! steady!
　'Tis pity we're so late.'

The boat lay off a barge beside,
　Nearer it could not draw,
(The Thames is deep, and very wide!)
　This Sambo watched, and saw

Full well that Harry could not leap
　With safety to the boat.—
The tide was high, the bank was steep,
　Huge timbers lay afloat!

Quick Harry forward sprung, so light,
　The other boys to meet,
But fell—head foremost! awful sight!
　For upward came his feet!

Poems from Adelaide

The boys shrieked loudly—far the sound
  Of ' Save him !' now was heard
They thought poor Harry surely drowned.
  Still, ' Save him !' was the word.—

For jammed between the timbers large
  The boy had disappeared,
And *sucked* beneath the weighty barge,
  Most probably, they feared.

But Sambo all the time stood by,
  When boat and boys arrived—
Straight, when he heard their fearful cry,
  Tho' dressed, he ran and dived !

Down in the river long remained ,
  But, oh, what shouts of joy,
When Sambo rose,—for he had gained
  The half-drowned senseless boy !

Into the house he quickly ran—
  Harry recovered slowly :
But from that hour he loved this man,
  Tho' black—in station lowly :

So proud and arrogant before,
  He now became most kind .
Called SAMBO '*black slave*' never more,
  Danger improved his mind

He now says, ' SAMBO, please do that ;'
  Or ' This or that pray do.'
Thus mutual good-will is of late,
  Observed between the two.

The Boasting Girl

YOUNG Agnes was a naughty girl,
  She seldom spoke the truth,
Was fond of *boasting* to her friends,
  A shameful fault in youth ;
      And every age—be it confessed—
      To speak the truth is ever best

She was a sly and artful one,
  Yet headstrong, wilful, wild ;
Her mother spoilt her—I much fear
  She was an only child !
      Mamma said, ' Agnes, willingly
      You may invite your friends to tea

' To-morrow evening they may come,
  Five girls, or six—not more,
In the large drawing-room you'll play,
  And fix the hour—say four.—
      It is not cold—you'll but require
      The lighted lamp .—not any fire

' But dear mamma the room *is* cold,
  A fire pray let us have.'
' No, Agnes, no,—alone you'll be,
  I must from peril save
      My little girl and her young friends
      For danger ever fire attends.

' You'll sing, and dance, and play about,
  Safely the spacious floor ,
The windows tight are fasten'd down,
  But *open* leave the door .—
      As I'm not well, I stay away ;
      Whilst you enjoy your evening pla.
373

Poems from Adelaide

The evening came—and first of all
  Thus Agnes disobeyed ,
Instead of six at most—there came,
  (In charming dress arrayed)
    Full *twelve* young girls by invitation !—
    Mamma show'd little approbation .

But to the drawing-room sent all,
  Where tea and cakes were ready.—
Then danced—piano played—and sung,
  Each nappy little lady !
    Play went on well—'till Agnes cried,
    ' Now all we want's a bright fireside !'

' No, no,' they said, ' we are not cold,
  But warm and in a glow !'
' But I am cold,' she quick replies,
  ' A fire I'll not forego—
    See ! here are lucifers, to light
    Our fire ! I hid them out of sight.',

' Stay, Agnes, stay !' the eldest cried ;
  ' Perhaps no fire has been
In this large room for many months—
  No signs of fire are seen !
    'Tis very true the *fire is laid*,
    But still to light it be afraid.'

' Afraid of what !' bold Agnes asked ;
  ' Sure here we *always* live,
And in this grate have fires so bright—
  My word you might believe !'
    Now this was *false*, as soon you'll hear ;
    The children looked at her with fear.

The Boasting Girl

She shut the door, applied the match,
  Oh, how the shavings blazed !
The smoke poured down—a thick black cloud
  The young ones screamed amazed :
     All blinded—choked—they ran about,
     With one terrific, fearful shout !

Mamma and many servants came
  To see what was the matter,
Out rushed the children, one and all,
  The servants ran for water
     To check the flames which widely spread !
     Agnes with fear was nearly dead.

'You wicked girl !' her mother cried ;
  ' You *will* then have your way !
That grate has had no fire for months,
  The chimney's stopped with hay !
     My dears, at once I'll send you home,
     And near that *lying* child again pray never
       come.'

Poems from Adelaide

Rachel's Sweet-Pease

'MY pretty sweet-pease, do not droop !
    Why do your lovely pink-buds stoop
        Thus lowly to the ground ?
Myself I sowed the seeds you know ,
To shoot up high you've not been slow,
And now you clustering grow,
    No sweeter flowers are found !

' Then why thus fall upon the earth ?
'Tis true, that was your place of birth,
    For from the earth you sprang,
But now you must expand upright,
And look fresh blooming to the sight,
Giving to all such sweet delight ''
    Thus to her flowers fair Rachel sang.

The flowers were deaf to Rachel's voice ;
What could they do ?—they had no choice
    But on the ground to lie !
Nor props nor kind support had they,—
With their own weight they fell—and lay
In wild confusion, all astray,
    Ready to pine and die !

The gardener saw her deep concern,
And much the reason wished to learn,
    Altho' he guessed it shrewdly ,
Rachel he never could entice
To take from him some good advice,
For she in flowers was over-nice,
    And sent him off most rudely '

Rachel's Sweet-Pease

' They want no sticks, I tell you, BEN,
I'll have no props, I say again,
 How ugly they would look !
Sweet-William has no prop, you see,
And wherefore stick up my sweet-pea ?
Pray leave my flower-beds all to me ;
 Advice I cannot brook.'

By slugs, by snails, by drenching showers,
Were crushed, full soon, her *prostrate* flowers !
 She mourned her loss too late !
Old Ben said, ' Lady, come this way ;
Here is *my* stand of sweet-pease gay ;
Accept them all, Miss Rachel, pray,
 They're yours, at any rate.'

And what met Rachel's joyful eyes,
Filling her heart with glad surprise,
 Stands of sweet-pease six feet high !
Loaded with blossoms here and there,
All firmly propped with tender care ;
The stalks were full—not one was bare,—
 She thought on hers with many a sigh

' You see, Miss Rachel,' said the man,
(Touching his hat, ere he began,)
 ' A different culture flowers must meet .
Some creep on earth—and some aspire
To rise—some high—some higher !
They then much skill and care require
 To well support their tender blossoms swee

Rachel, enchanted, now no longer sighs,
But visits daily her fair blooming prize '

Rather too Good, Little Peggy !

A TRUE STORY

'OH, pray come in,
  Mamma's within,
Pray do not stay out there,
It pours with rain,
I say again
  Come in, and take a chair.'
Thus lisped little PEGGY, whilst holding the door,
To a poor ragged woman she'd ne'er seen before !

' Mamma's up stairs,
She always cares
  For children that are poor,
Come in, I pray,
Out there don't stay,   .
  For I must shut the door '
In walked three poor children, all squalid and mean,
Whom PEGGY, so courteous, till now had not seen

'Mamma, come down !
I'm not alone,
  I've asked them to come in,
I heard the knock,
Undid the lock :
  Here's bread, so pray begin.'

Mamma came down, and stood amazed '
  Whether to laugh, or angry be,
  She knew not well,
  And could not tell,
Till on the group she gazed,
  And thus the truth could see.

378

Rather too Good, Little Peggy!

'Indeed, my lady, do believe,'
  The woman humbly said.
Mamma replied, 'Take all the bread ;
  To see such misery I grieve,—
But must not let my child do thus,
  She is not four years old.
I'll give you money, clothes, a few,
  To shelter these from cold.'

The woman thanked the lady kind,
  And gratefully went out,
But Peggy could not comprehend,
  What this was all about !
'Why, dear mamma, was I not right,
  To ask them in to stay all night ?'
'My child, your heart is understood ,
  (How can I well explain !)
When indiscreet—we're call'd TOO GOOD.'
  Never do so again.

Poems from Adelaide

The Alarum Bell

'PRAY let us have some peace,
  Talking you'll never cease;
I ne'er knew one so young
Gifted with such a tongue !

' I really think of late
You love to hear your prate !
But be at once assured
This habit shall be cured.'

  Still Caroline talk'd away
  To her doll, as if in play ;
  To chattering no end !
  Until this same kind friend
Thus taught the young girl to obey.

At the top of the house there hung
  A large alarum bell ;
When pull'd, its *tongue* loud sung !
  'Twould answer very well
Of thieves, or fire, to give the alarm,
And save the inmates all from harm.

  *   *   *   *

  Mamma one morning chose
  To see some friends—when soon arose
  A clamouring little voice !
For *loudly* to prattle was Caroline's choice.
  And thus the noise
  Their peace destroys,
While about the room she flings her toys.

The Alarum Bell

' You love me, little doll, don't *you* ?
That I love doll is very true,
  Shall I my dolly dress ?
I'll kiss your cheeks, I'll curl your hair ;
You are like me so very fair,
  My doll I must caress !

 ' My dolly has a pretty bed
 Altho' my dolly is not fed,
She never grows much thinner,
  But in my mind,
  If she's inclined,
Would not refuse a dinner.'

This more than childish nonsense was
 Repeated once or twice,
But, hark ! what dreadful peal is that
 Loud sounded in a trice ?
 The alarum bell is rung,
 Which never rang before !
 Oh, listen to its brazen tongue
 In rapid lengthened roar !

The noisy prattler was struck dumb !
 Mamma's fond arms she seeks,
In real terror at the sound.—
 Papa thus gravely speaks ·—

' This is to cure your naughty ways ;
 To idle chatter bid farewell,—
When loud and troublesome you get,
 I ring the alarum bell.'

Poems from Adelaide

The Organ Boy and Lord Augustus

'NO wonder you are thin, you organ boy,
　　　Idling about all day with such a load,
You stun my ears ! pray don't our house annoy—
　　What brings you here?—why came you from
　　　　abroad ?

' The lad, tho' poor, yet smiles—he looks not well.
　　He is not ragged, tho' he seems ill-fed !
But nothing, that I see, he has to sell—
　　Well, here, poor organ boy, here is a loaf of bread.

' How's this ! refuse my kindly offer'd gift !
　　Then wherefore grind your music in our ears ?
From off our walk your organ-stick play lift,
　　You are not hungry—why, what mean your tears?'

' Ah, Signor,* Signor—English me no speak.'
　　Augustus with contempt drove him away,
The duchess quickly called the poor boy back,
　　And gravely told him a sweet tune to play

A shilling then she gave him with a smile,
　　He bowed, and happy left the charming place.
Augustus, greatly wondering, watched the while,
　　And sought her meaning in his mother's face

' First then, my son, you *idle* called the boy,
　　And yet 'tis music gains his daily bread.
What brought him here, you next inquired—DECOY !
　　From Italy with others he was led—

* Sir
382

The Organ Boy

' With cruel purpose—sold I greatly fear
  By parents (who a parent's feelings lack,)
To men most griping, stern, severe—
  Money to them at night boys *must* bring back.

' If not, they're scolded, punished, knocked about.—
  This was the cause your *bread* he did not take,
My dear Augustus, now the secret's out ;
  Tho' he refused, I thought his little heart would
    break.'

The youth was silent long, and then observed,
  ' *My* gift was his, *yours* to the master went :
And is not this encouragement absurd
  To those Decoys who with such bad intent

' Take these poor lads from Italy and home,
  Organs to grind, mice, guinea-pigs to show ?
Sending them all thro' foreign parts to roam ·
  Our senators humane these truths should know.'

' The time may come when *you* will have the power,
  In Parliament, this evil to abate.
Augustus, then, look back upon this hour,
  When thus explained the organ boy's sad fate.'

All Wrong

A T a poor crippled person to mock,
   Or mimic a stuttering tongue,
A cradle to wantonly rock:
By shrieking, a sick one to shock—
   Is certainly wicked and wrong.

To titter and laugh in the church,
   Or rattle with half-pence, ding dong,
To leave a blind man in the lurch,
To Threaten a baby with birch,—
   All this you'll confess is most wrong.

To cut a poor boy's flying kite,
   To ask a dumb girl for a song,
To set on your playmates to fight,
To deprive a poor bird of its sight,—
   Is cruel, and savage, and wrong.

To stone a poor horse, or a cow,
   To *fag* a young lad, 'cause *you're* strong,
To the blind make a mischievous bow,
Rob gardens, and call it 'fine Row!'—
   All this we condemn as most wrong.

I hope my young friends, one and all,
   Such boys never venture among,
Altho' they be rich, fair, and tall—
If they do, they will certainly fall
   From RIGHT, into what is most WRONG.

All Right

TO lend a poor cripple your arm
   In assisting the blind with *your* sight,
To shield the young child from all harm,
To love the sweet country and farm,—
   Is surely most good and quite right.

Attention to study at school,
   And fairly your copies to write,—
Your wishes and temper to rule,
In silence to pass a rude fool;
   All this we deem perfectly right.

In paying respect to old age,
   And praying both morning and night,
In reading the blest sacred page,—
All this do, and we may engage,
   That ever you'll follow the right.

To save a poor animal found,
   Or lamed, or deprived of its sight,
To feed a starved horse in the pound,
To lift a poor babe from the ground,—
   We really say this is right.

I hope my young readers attend
   With great, and sincerest delight,
(When a diligent ear they lend,)
To this the advice of a friend,—
   Then truly we're all in the right.

D D

Appendix IV

Four of the Original Fables at the
end of ' Æsop in Rhyme '
by Jefferys Taylor

The Donkeys' Dialogue

'TWAS in a shady, cool retreat,
    Two friendly donkeys chanced to meet,
Who, resting from a tedious walk,
Laid down, and soon began to talk.

' Well met,' said one—' good morning, brother !'
' Aha ! good morning,' said the other ;
—' A cloudy day—shall we have thunder ?'
' Sir,' said his friend, ' I should not wonder;
The cattle seem for shelter going,
The sheep are bleating, cows are lowing,
The frogs are croaking, geese are wheezing,
Pigs are grunting, cats are sneezing,
And as for me, I'm well aware,
There must be something in the air ,
For I've got such a cold to-day,
And am so hoarse, I can scarce bray.'

' Well,' said the other, ' who'd have thought it ;
Surely this south-west wind has brought it ;
For *I've* a cold, but I suppose
Mine must have settled in my nose ;

The Donkeys' Dialogue

For I've entirely lost my smell,
Although I *bray* exceeding well.'

' Ah !' said his friend, ' beyond dispute,
A donkey's nerves are more acute
Than those of men, who ne'er foresee
A thunder-storm so soon as we ;
And don't you think although we're asses,
Our *sense* and *reason* their's surpasses ?'

' Why don't you know,' his friend replied,
' Our reason is by them denied ,
When told of brute's sagacity,
They have the strange audacity
To say 'tis *instinct*, and maintain
We've nothing else to guide our brain !
Yet brutes do nothing half so silly
As I've seen done by *Master Billy* ;
I've known him go and tie the grass
Across the way where people pass ,
Or push his play-mates in the dirt,
Not caring much if they were hurt.
This the sole object of his labours,
To please himself and plague his neighbours.
'Twas not ten days ago I think,
As I was stooping down to drink,
His *sense* and *reason* to discover,
He needs must turn the water over ;
Now was this wise or was it not ?
Pray was it reason, sense, or what ?
If it was *reason*, there's no doubt
'Tis better far to be without ,
And if 'twas *instinct*, then I say,
We have a *better sort* than they ,
But I'm convinced these actions shew
That they have *neither* ot the two.

387

Peter the Great

A CERTAIN man, as some do say,
    Who lived in peace and quiet,
Did line his inside every day
    With most nutritious diet.

' For sure,' thought he, as skilfully
    The mutton he did carve,
' 'Twould be exceeding wrong in me
    My body for to starve.'

His body, measured round about,
    When his great coat was on,
Was four good yards, there's not a doubt,
    His weight was forty stone

Peter the Great, I do aver,
    He was without pretence,
Judging from his diameter,
    And his circumference.

No wonder then this Briton bold
    To stir him should be loth ;
His arms reluctant he would fold ;
    His legs unwilling both.

And yet his loving wife would say,
    ' Peter, thou art to blame ;
Thou didst not stir out yesterday,
    To-day 'tis all the same.'

  ' Ah ! Judith, dear, I doubt,' said he,
    ' My stirring days are past ·
For don't ye know, and don't ye see,
    My shadow lengthens fast.'

Peter the Great

'Not so,' quoth Judith, 'if I'm right,
   Thou surely must be wrong ;
Thy shadow seems unto my sight
   As broad as it is long '

Thus pleasantly, to make him glad,
   She answered him alway,
Till he at last, with sorrow sad,
   Unto his wife did say :

'Judith, I am not well at all,
   Within I'm sore distrest ;
I fear I'm ill with what they call
   A load upon my chest.

'I know not when I've felt so bad ;
   I think, say what you will,
That goose that yesterday I had
   Is in my stomach still !

'Haste for the doctor, ere he's out,
   For he may be of use ;
Tell him my feet have got the gout,
   My stomach's got the goose.'

The dame approved her husband's thought,
   As heretofore she did ,
For long ago she had been taught
   To do as she was bid.

Said she, ' I go , but it may be
   Some time I shall be gone ;
So 'twill be better first for me
   To put the boiler on.

'For if by reason of your pain
   To fast be good for you,
It does not follow hence 'tis plain
   That I must famish too.'

The dame then sped her on her way,
  And jogged for many a mile;
And Peter he at home did stay,
  To mind the pot the while.

But in his chair of ample size
  While seated, I suppose,
This trusty watch did shut his eyes,
  And straight began to doze.

At last the water, heated hot,
  Lifted the cauldron's cover,
And then (as cooks affirm) *the pot*
  Did boil with fury over.

Water and fire with angry strife,
  A hissing dire did make;
Which Peter hearing, dreamed his wife
  Was broiling him a steak.

But as the hissing still kept on,
  He dreamed she'll surely spoil it;
Then gruffly growled, 'The meat is done,
  How long d'ye mean to boil it?'

Then in his dream his sleepy poll
  With anger great did nod he,
When lo! the tumult of his soul
  Awoke his peaceful body.

Then loudly to his wife he called,
  'Come hither, dame, I pray!'
But vainly to the dame he bawled,
  For she was far away.

At last he reached his walking-stick
  To shove the boiling-pot,
When o'er his legs it tumbled quick!
  And water scalding hot!

Peter the Great

Up went his feet into the air;
   Down went his body great;
Crack went the ancient elbow chair!
   And eke poor Peter's pate!

No longer now he felt the gout,
   But, roaring out amain,
Briskley he turned his legs about,
   And stood upright again.

With scalded feet and broken head,
   He danced along the floor;
He had not done the like 'tis said,
   For twenty years or more.

Then round the room the woful wight
   Did cast a mournful eye;
Thought he, 'I'm in a dismal plight,
   That none can well deny.'

There prostrate lay the broken chair,
   The boiler on the ground
The cat, she thought her fate severe,
   To be both scalt and drowned.

But now his wife's return from town
   Full sore began to dread he;
Thought he, 'She'd surely crack my crown,
   Were it not cracked already'

But long he waited all forlorn,
   With pining discontent,
And still his wife did not return,
   Although the day was spent.

At last the street-door lock within
   The key began to rattle;
Thought Peter, 'Now will soon begin
   A most tremendous battle.'

Jefferys Taylor's Poems

Then, with the doctor close behind,
   Entered the wife of Peter ;
But how was she surprised to find
   Her husband came to meet her.

Said she, ' How's this, that thou *alone*
   Canst walk along the path ?'
Said he, ' I've been, since thou wast gone,
   In a *hot water bath*.'

Now Peter he began to quake,
   As Judith entered in ;
Who, when she saw the mess, did make
   A most surprising din.

' Woman, I've broke my head,' said he,
   ' And *scalt* my legs to boot ;
So sure there is no need for thee
   To add affliction to 't.'

But ' said the doctor, ' tell me, sir,
   How 'tis you walk about ,
Your wife affirmed you could not stir,
   By reason of the gout.'

Then Peter he related quite
   What we have told before ,
Then did the doctor laugh outright,
   With loud and lengthened roar

' But, sir,' said he, ' now I suppose,
   That, all this time you've fasted
Pray tell me if your stomach's woes
   The same till now have lasted.'

' Why, sir,' said Peter, ' I must own
   That, since from food I've rested,
The load is from my stomach gone,
   And seems to be digested.'

Peter the Great

'Then,' said the doctor, 'I advise
    When plagued with gouty pain,
Since that's removed by exercise,
    To scald your legs again.

'And as you'd find your health increased,
    Were you but somewhat thinner;
I charge you twice a week at least
    To go without your dinner.'

Thus I, at last, have sung my song,
    With no small care and trouble;
So, as the fable has been long,
    The moral shall be double.

And first, when, through excess of food,
    You find your stomach ill,
Then abstinence will do more good
    Than bolus, draught, or pill.

Again, when pain in limbs comes on
    So you can scarce endure it;
Then jump about—'tis ten to one
    But exercise will cure it.

Jefferys Taylor's Poems

The Show of Wild Beasts

TWO apes exhibited for show,
  Some time by *Mr. Polito*,
Thinking their master did not need 'em,
Determined to obtain their freedom ,
So waiting till the coast was clear,
One day, when nobody was near,
They issued forth, and hand in hand.
Walked for an airing down the Strand ,
Nor were they presently espied,
Among so many apes beside ;
But unmolested passed along
Amid the numerous monkey throng ;
Both making sundry observations,
On those they thought were their relations.

At last they formed the bold design
Some *human* monkeys to confine,
And show them off (so says the fable)
As English apes, if they were able
And so it seems, by hook or crook,
Six curious animals they took,
And putting instantly to sea,
They soon arrived in *Barbary*
Among their friends, and let them know
They'd got some foreign beasts to show
These friends so thronged the exhibition,
That many could not gain admission
Our apes with joy the concourse viewed,
And made for all what room they could ;
And then, as is the usual plan,
They took their wands, and thus began.

The Show of Wild Beasts

'Good friends and neighbours all : you see
After long absence here we are :
We have at last our freedom gained,
Though fourteen years we've been detained,
By apes of an inferior sort
Exhibited, to make them sport ;
Of whom we've now kidnapped a few,
To make in turn some sport for you.

'First you behold the English glutton,
He feeds on beef, pork, veal, and mutton ,
But, Oh ! such dinners he devours ,—
His mouth holds twice as much as our's ,
At once he in his stomach puts
The worth of half a sack of nuts ;
But, what is singular indeed,
He never knows *how long* to feed ;
But when no longer hungry will,
While food remains, keep eating still .
He'll prove the truth of what I've said,
If you'll but stay, and see him fed.

'Here,' said the showman, 'you behold
An odd young monkey, nine years old ;
At least, as near as I can guess
From size and strength, he can't be less,
Although were you his ways to see,
You'd say he was not turned of three ,
I think, his name they told me once,
'Tis, if I don't mistake, *a dunce.*
Now, from this creature it appears
Boys' wits increase not with their years ;
A striking difference, indeed,
'Twixt them and us, but let's proceed.

'The English sloth you there may see ;
As usual, sound asleep is he ;

Jefferys Taylor's Poems

You'll scarce believe me when I say
He sleeps all night, and half the day !
'Tis ten or twelve before he'll rise,
And hardly then can ope his eyes ;
I fear that now we shall not wake him,
Unless one goes inside to shake him ;
But while asleep you best behold
All that about him can be told.

' This creature here in sickness pines ;
We do not understand his signs.
What 'tis he wants we cannot tell,
We never could when he was well ;
He says he's hungry : but, the fact is,
To say that is his constant practice ,
A form of speech he uses then
Peculiar to the race of men ;
I can't explain it, no, not I,
But think 'tis what *they* call a *lie.*

' This is an English ape full grown,
The first for your amusement shown ,
I fear you will not understand me,
When I pronounce his name, a *dandy* :
Vast numbers of this race of apes
I've seen in town of various shapes ;
Their brains are few, as you may guess,
For, all their thoughts they spend on dress ;
O ! stop, not *all*, how fast I'm talking ,
For tired of riding, tired of walking,
And wishing much for something new,
They thought they would combine the two,
And tried to speed them on the road,
While they that odd machine bestrode ,

The Show of Wild Beasts

You see this thing we've brought away ;*
—Come! show the company, I say.

' This animal, with doubled fist,
Is what they call a *pugilist;*
A most uncommon creature, Sirs !
Has changed his *generic characters;*
A beast Linnæus never saw ;
No cutting teeth in either jaw,
Though nature gave him some, no doubt ;
But now you see they all are out.
His eyes once grey, as I suppose,
You now perceive are black as sloes ;
His nose, once straight, you see is broken ;
His features cruelty betoken ·
He is, I think, to say the least,
A frightful and disgusting beast

' Thus, neighbours, we have shown you all
The beasts we've taken, great and small ;
Full twenty more were on their way,
Whom we could not compel to stay :
Indeed, we got such blows and kicks,
The wonder is we mustered six.
They're few indeed, we freely own,
Out of the hundreds we have known ;
But yet enough, we feel persuaded,
To show that men are *apes* degraded '

* A velocipede, the earliest form of the bicycle —ED

The Shower of Puddings

SAID a youth to the clouds, as he turned up his
    eyes,
'How I wish soup and pudding were rained from the
    skies!
O! how charming 'twould be ready cooked if 'twould
    fall,
That so one might dine with no trouble at all.'

And so it fell out, says the fable, at last
That the sky with some odd looking clouds was o'ercast,
And the south wind blew up a most savoury smell,
When direct from the heavens the aliments fell!

Now the pea-soup and pudding descended amain,
Till it poured from the mountains and deluged the plain,
The pigs were astonished ; yet did not forget,
Like our youth, while they wondered, that now they
    might eat.

'However,' thought he, 'I will benefit by it ;'
So he took up a piece of plum-pudding to try it ;
But, alas, he could not even swallow a bit,
For he found it was covered with gravel and grit.

Who'd have thought it, when pudding was rained from
    the skies,
That it yet would be needful some plan to devise,
And *some* trouble to take to accomplish his wish ;
For *now*, ere he dined, *he must hold up his dish.*

The Shower of Puddings

But this dish was not filled quite so soon as he thought,
So that both his arms ached ere enough he had caught;
But something soon happened, more dismal by half,
At which you'll have too much good nature to laugh;

For a large piece of pudding, of more than a pound,
Knocked the dish from the hands of our youth to the
    ground.
' Well,' said he, ' I have played long enough at this
    game,
Let it rain what it will, it comes all to the same;
Good things, how abundant soever they be,
One can never obtain without trouble, I see.'

A Few Notes

Page 5.—' A True Story.'

When Kate Greenaway made an illustrated edition of a selection of the *Original Poems*—one of her most charming books—she gave it the title, *Little Ann and Her Mother*, by which name the ' True Story' is indeed generally known. So many people are familiar with the earlier version of this poem that, although the changes are not numerous or important, I give it here. I reproduce also Isaac Taylor's illustration from one of the earliest editions, concerning which Mr. Henry Taylor, the son of the artist, and nephew of Ann and Jane, writes to me very interestingly as follows · ' My father has brought out in his sketch the strong contrast between the *personæ dramatis* When I was a boy walking about London fifty years ago, the carriages of the nobility were greatly more ostentatious than at present, and the servants had powdered hair, silk stockings, gold braid, etc. ; but fifty years before that time the contrast was much more marked. My father was then a young artist living in London, and he sketched very graphically exactly what he saw. Many modern artists only put in a coachman and two footmen, while their clothes are not those of the period, and Ann's mother is made quite grand enough to have been the occupant of the carriage. My father has given a picture of the six men-servants usually employed by the nobility on such occasions. There is (*a*) the postillion, with gold-braided jacket and cap, (*b*) the coachman, of course not holding any reins, and with a grander hat than that worn by the (*c*) two footmen standing up behind. There are then (*d*) the two footmen handing the grand lady into her coach. Then, again, Ann and her mother are wearing a suitable middle-class costume.'

Little Ann and her Mother.
(From the illustration designed and engraved by Isaac Taylor.)

A TRUE STORY.

LITTLE Ann and her mother were walking one day
   Thro' London's wide city so fair ;
And bus'ness oblig'd them to go by the way
   That led them through Cavendish Square.

A Few Notes

And as they pass'd by the great house of a lord,
  A beautiful chariot there came,
To take some most elegant ladies abroad,
  Who straightway got into the same.

The ladies in feathers and jewels were seen,
  The chariot was painted all o'er,
The footmen behind were in silver and green,
  The horses were prancing before

Little Ann by her mother walk'd silent and sad,
  A tear trickled down from her eye ;
Till her mother said, 'Ann, I should be very glad
  To know what it is makes you cry'

'Mamma,' said the child, 'see that carriage so fair,
  All cover'd with varnish and gold,
Those ladies are riding so charmingly there,
  While we have to walk in the cold .

'You say GOD is kind to the folks that are good,
  But surely it cannot be true;
Or else I am certain, almost, that he would
  Give such a fine carriage to you'

'Look there, little girl,' said her mother, 'and see
  What stands at that very coach door ,
A poor ragged beggar, and listen how she
  A halfpenny stands to implore.

'All pale is her face, and deep sunk is her eye,
  Her hands look like skeleton's bones ,
She has got a few rags just about her to tie,
  And her naked feet bleed on the stones'

'Dear ladies,' she cries, and the tears trickle down,
  'Relieve a poor beggar, I pray ,
I've wander'd all hungry about this wide town,
  And not eat a morsel to-day

'My father and mother are long ago dead,
  My brother sails over the sea ,
And I've not a rag, or a morsel of bread,
  As plainly, I'm sure, you may see.

'A fever I caught, which was terribly bad,
  But no nurse or physic had I ,
An old dirty shed was the house that I had,
  And only on straw could I lie,

'And now that I'm better, yet feeble, and faint,
   And famish'd, and naked, and cold,
I wander about, with my grievous complaint,
   And seldom get aught but a scold

'Some will not attend to my pitiful call,
   Some think me a vagabond cheat ;
And scarcely a creature relieves me, of all
   The thousands that traverse the street.

'Then ladies, dear ladies, your pity bestow ,'——
   Just then a tall footman came round,
And asking the ladies which way they would go,
   The chariot turn'd off with a bound

- 'Ah ! see, little girl,' then her mother replied,
   ' How foolish it was to complain ,
If you would but have look'd at the contrary side,
   Your tears would have dried up again.

'Your house, and your friends, and your victuals, and bed,
   'Twas GOD in His mercy that gave ·
You did not deserve to be cover'd and fed,
   Yet all of these blessings you have

'This poor little beggar is hungry and cold,
   No father or mother has she ;
And while such an object as this you behold,
   Contented, indeed, you should be

'A coach, and a footman, and gaudy attire,
   Give little true joy to the breast ,
To be good is the thing you should chiefly desire,
   And then leave to GOD all the rest'

Page 43.—'The Boys and the Apple-Tree.'

In the original edition William and Thomas were
called Billy and Tommy. Benjamin Green was called
Bobby Green, and he anticipated not 'a most happy
day,' but 'a rare jolly day ' Man-traps are no longer
used for little boys in England.

Page 51 —' Idle Richard and the Goats.'

Richard was originally called Dicky

A Few Notes

Page 54.—'George and the Chimney-Sweep.'

In the final edition this poem was reduced and altered.
I quote, from the edition of 1812, Adelaide's verses as they
were written

GEORGE AND THE CHIMNEY-SWEEPER.

HIS petticoats now George cast off,
  For he was four years old ;
His trowsers were nankeen so fine,
  His buttons bright as gold —
' May I,' said little George, ' go out,
  My pretty clothes to show ?
May I, papa ? may I, mamma ?'
  The answer was—' No, no.'

' Go run below, George, in the court,
  But go not in the street,
Lest naughty boys should play some trick,
  Or gipsies you should meet.'
Yet tho' forbade, George went unseen
  That other boys might spy ,
And all admir'd him when he lisp'd—
  ' Now who so fine as I ?'

But whilst he strutted to and fro,
  So proud, as I've heard tell,
A sweep-boy pass'd, whom to avoid
  He slipp'd, and down he fell.
The sooty lad was kind and good,
  To Georgy boy he ran,
He rais'd him up, and kissing said,
  ' Hush, hush, my little man !'

He rubb'd and wip'd his clothes with care,
  And hugging said, ' Don't cry '—
Go home, as quick as you can go
  Sweet little boy, good-bye '
Poor George look'd down, and lo ' his dress
  Was blacker than before ,
All over soot, and mud, and dirt,
  He reach'd his father's door

He sobb'd, and wept, and look'd asham'd,
  His fault he did not hide :
And since so sorry for his fault,
  Mamma forbore to chide.

404

A Few Notes

That night when he was gone to bed,
　He jump'd up in his sleep,
And cried and sobb d, and cried again,
　'I thought I saw the sweep !'

Page 62.—' The Plum-Cake.'

In its original form this little ballad had more vigour.
I quote the text of 1812 :

THE PLUM CAKE.

'OH ! I've got a plum cake, and a rare feast I'll make,
　I'll eat, and I'll stuff, and I'll cram,
Morning, noontime, and night, it shall be my delight,
　What a happy young fellow I am.'

Thus said little George, and beginning to gorge,
　With zeal to his cake he applied ;
While fingers and thumbs, for the sweetmeats and plums,
　Were hunting and digging beside.

But woful to tell, a misfortune befel,
　Which ruin'd this capital fun ;
After eating his fill, he was taken so ill,
　That he trembled for what he had done.

As he grew worse and worse, the doctor and nurse,
　To cure his disorder were sent .
And rightly, you ll think, he had physic to drink,
　Which made him his folly repent

And while on the bed he roll d his hot head,
　Impatient with sickness and pain,
He could not but take this reproof from his cake ·
　' Don't be such a glutton again '

Page 75.—' My Mother.'

It is, perhaps, no exaggeration to say that this is the
best-known English poem. I give on the next and the
following page two drawings made to illustrate it by
Isaac Taylor, the author's brother

I have omitted, on p. 76, the last stanza of this poem
in its early form This stanza, as it then ran, was objected
to on sound doctrinal grounds by the late Augustus de

A Few Notes

Morgan, the mathematician, in a letter to the *Athenæum* in 1866. Mr. de Morgan, who was not aware that Mrs. Gilbert (Ann Taylor) was alive, remarked at the end of his communication: 'We propose that it [the poem] should be remitted to the Laureate, in the name of all the children of England, to supply a closing verse which shall give a motive drawn from the verses which precede, and in accordance with the one immediately pre-

ceding. It will not be easy, even for Mr. Tennyson, to satisfy reasonable expectation : but we hope he will try.' The next week Mrs. Gilbert replied, pointing out that she was still living, expressing agreement with her critic, and undertaking to make an alteration. The revised stanza ran :

> For could our Father in the skies
> Look down with pleased or loving eyes,
> If ever I could dare despise
> My Mother ?

À Few Notes

Page 82.—' The Fox and the Crow.'

Supposed by Mr. Arthur Hall to be by Bernard Barton, the Quaker Poet

Page 91.—' James and the Shoulder of Mutton.'

The incident told here really occurred to one of the young Dartons, the children of the publisher of *Original Poems.*

Page 114.—' Creation.'

Said by Mr Arthur Hall to be by Isaac Taylor, the brother of Ann and Jane.

Page 116.—' The Tempest.'

Also by Ann and Jane Taylor's brother, Isaac

Page 177.—' The Cow and the Ass.'

I quote from the *Spectator* the following interesting criticism of this very agreeable fable 'To the present writer the gem of Jane Taylor's work, and, indeed, of all the *Original Poems*, is her playful little apologue, " The Cow and the Ass." For charming grace and comic humour it has seldom been surpassed. The picture of the two friendly animals by the stream, among the daisies and grass, is as cool and refreshing as a good water-colour drawing. Their manners are most elegant ; the cow's complaint has an air of melancholy reason ; the " brown Ass, of respectable look," argues with her like a true philosopher—

> With submission, dear Madam, to your better wit—

and she, though convinced by his wisdom, has a feminine unwillingness to acknowledge it :

> The cow, upon this, cast her eyes on the grass,
> Not pleased at thus being reproved by an ass.

La Fontaine himself could not have done it much better, and in the case of no other writer for children, we think, could such a comparison even be suggested.'

A Few Notes

Page 202.—' Frances keeps her Promise '

In the early editions this piece ran rather differently
I quote from the text of 1813.

FRANCES KEEPS HER PROMISE

' My Fanny, I have news to tell,
  Your diligence quite pleases me,
You've work'd so neatly, read so well,
  With cousin Jane you may drink tea

' But pray, my dear, remember this,
  Altho' to stay you should incline,
Tho' warmly press'd by each kind Miss,
  I wish you to return by nine '

With many thanks th' attentive child
  Assur'd mamma she would obey :
When wash'd and dress'd she kiss'd and smil'd,
  And with the maid she went away.

When reach'd her cousin's, she was shown
  To where her little friends were met,
And when her coming was made known,
  Around her flock'd the cheerful set.

They dance, they play and sweetly sing,
  In ev'ry sport each child partakes,
And now the servants sweetmeats bring,
  With wine and jellies, fruit and cakes.

In comes papa, and says —' My dears,
  The magic lantern if you'd see,
And that which on the wall appears,
  Leave off your play, and follow me '

Whilst Frances too enjoy'd the sight,
  Where moving figures all combine,
To raise her wonder and delight,
  She hears the parlour clock strike nine.

The boy walks in : ' Miss Ann is come,'—
  ' O dear how soon " the children cry ;
They press, but Fanny will go home,
  And bids her little friends good-bye.

A Few Notes

'My dear mamma, am I not good?'
 'You are indeed,' mamma replies ;
But when you said, I thought you wou'd
 Return, and thus you've won a prize

' This way, my love, and see the man
 Whom I desir'd at nine to call.'—
Down stairs young Frances quickly ran,
 And found him waiting in the hall.

' Here, Miss, are pretty birds to buy,
 A parrot or maccaw so gay ;
A speckled dove with scarlet eye,
 But quickly choose, I cannot stay.

' Would you a Java sparrow love ?'
 ' No, no, I thank you,' said the child ;
' I'll have a beauteous cooing dove,
 So harmless, innocent, and mild '

' Your choice, my Fanny, I commend,
 Few birds can with the dove compare ,
But, lest it pine without a friend,
 You may, my dear, choose out a pair.'

Page 212.—' The Linnet's Nest.'

Ann and Jane Taylor wrote together a little book in
verse, published in 1822, entitled *The Linnet's Life*, in
which, in a series of poems, they described the adventures
of a linnet which was given to a little girl and kept by
her in a cage : its narrow escape from the cat, and so
forth.

Page 233.—' The Gaudy Flower.'

Attributed by Mr. Arthur Hall to Isaac Taylor, father
of Ann and Jane Taylor.

A Few Notes

Page 234.—' Negligent Mary.'

This piece, also by Ann and Jane Taylor's father, was originally very different in form, and was called ' Sluttishness.' I copy below the version of 1813 :

SLUTTISHNESS.

AH ! Mary, my Mary, why where is your Dolly ?
    Look here, I protest, on the floor ;
To leave her about in the dirt so is folly,
    You ought to be trusted no more

I thought you were pleas'd, and receiv'd her quite gladly,
    When on your birth-day she came home ,
Did I ever suppose you would use her so sadly,
    And strew her things over the room

Her bonnet of straw you once thought a great matter,
    And tied it so pretty and neat ,
Now see how 'tis crumpled, no trencher is flatter,
    It grieves your mamma thus to see 't.

Suppose, (you're my Dolly, you know, little daughter,
    Whom I love to dress neat, and see good,)
Suppose in my care of you, I were to faulter,
    And let you get dirty and rude '

But Dolly's mere wood, you are flesh and blood living,
    And deserve better treatment and care ,
That is true, my sweet girl, tis the reason I m giving
    This lesson so sharp and severe.

'Tis not for the Dolly I'm anxious and fearful,
    Tho' she cost too much to be spoil'd ,
I'm afraid lest yourself should get sluttish, not careful
    And that were a sad thing, my child

A Few Notes

Page 252.—' Good-Night.'

The last stanza was rewritten. Originally the first
four lines prettily ran :

> For the curtains warm are spread
> Round about her cradle bed ,
> And her little night-cap hides
> Every breath of air besides

Page 262.—' The Star.'

This is, after ' My Mother,' probably the best known
of all the Taylors' poems.

Page 267.—' Poor Children.'

This little poem was greatly altered from the first
edition (1806), where it runs thus

POOR CHILDREN.

WHEN I go in the meadows, or walk in the street,
Very often a many poor children I meet,
Without shoes or stockings to cover their feet.

Their clothes are all ragged, and let in the cold ;
And they have very little to eat, I am told
Oh dear ! 'tis a pitiful sight to behold

And then, what is worse, very often they are
Quite naughty and wicked,—I never can bear
To hear how they quarrel together, and swear.

For often they use naughty words in their play ,
And I might have been quite as wicked as they,
If I'd not been taught better, I heard mamma say.

O how very thankful I always should be,
That I have kind parents to watch over me,
Who teach me from wickedness ever to flee !

And as mamma tells me, I certainly should
Mind all that is taught me, and be very good,
For if those poor children knew better, *they* would.

A Few Notes

Page 269.—' Of what are Your Clothes made ?'

In the third stanza the fur of the shy beaver was originally left out of the composition of the hat. The lines ran :

> And then the grey rabbit contributes his share ;
> He helps to provide you a hat.

Page 291.—' The Little Coward '

The last line of the third stanza was stronger in the original. It ran :

> But off the little booby hies

Page 293 —' The Little Boy who made Himself Ill.'

I quote the original version to show how thoroughly the piece was rewritten

THE SICK LITTLE BOY.

> Ah ! why's my sweet fellow so pale ?
>   And why do the little tears fall ?
> Come, tell me, love, what do you ail,
>   And mother shall cure him of all.
> There, lay your white cheek on my lap,
>   With your pin a-fore over your head,
> And perhaps, when you've taken a nap,
>   Again your white cheek may be red.
>
> O ! no, don t be kind to me yet
>   I do not deserve to be kiss'd ;
> Some gooseb'ries and currants I eat,
>   For I thought that they would not be miss'd ;
> And so, when you left me alone,
>   I took them, altho' they were green !
> But is it not better to own
>   What a sad naughty boy I have been ?
>
> O ! yes, I am sorry to hear
>   The thing that my Richard has done ;
> But as you have own'd it, my dear,
>   You have not made two faults of one :

413

A Few Notes

Be sure that you never again
  Forget that God watches your way,
And patiently bear with your pain,
  That does but your folly repay

Page 332.—' The Little Girl who was Naughty, and
who was afterwards very sorry for it.'

This poem, originally called ' Passion and Penitence,'
was practically rewritten.   I quote its first state:

PASSION AND PENITENCE.

HERE'S morning again, and a good fireside,
  And a breakfast so nice in a bason so full ;
How good, dear mamma, for my wants to provide,
  I ought to be good too—but sure you are dull

You don't smile to meet me, nor call me your dear ,
  Nor place your arms round me so kind on your knee ;
Nor give the sweet kiss, as I climb up your chair
  Nay, sure that's a frown, are you angry with me ?

Oh, now I remember,—quite naughty last night,
  I left you in passion, nor came for a kiss ,
I bounc'd from the room in vexation and spite
  Indeed 'twas ungrateful, I did act amiss.

My fretful ill temper, so naughty and rude,
  To you 'twas unkind, before God it was wrong .
I'm asham'd to come near, when I know I'm not good ·
  You ought not to kiss me for ever so long

Yet, indeed, I do love you, and stoutly will try
  To subdue ev'ry passion that moves me amiss :
I'll pray God to pardon my sin, lest I die
  When you see my repentance, I know you will kiss

Page 346.—' The Wedding among the Flowers.'

By Ann Taylor alone.   Published in 1808 in a little
paper-coloured book, with copper-plate pictures.   It was
Ann Taylor's very ingenious and fanciful contribution to
the new fashion in children's books, which began with

414

A Few Notes

Roscoe's *Butterfly's Ball* in 1807, and produced so many imitations, *The Peacock at Home*, by Mrs. Dorset, being the first and the best known.

Page 370.—'Harry, the Arrogant Boy, and Sambo.'

In the *Poetry for Children*, by Mary and Charles Lamb, published in 1809, there is a story of a similar character, called 'Conquest of Prejudice.'

Page 394.—'The Show of Wild Beasts.'

Mr. Polito kept a menagerie at Exeter Change, which stood, a hundred years ago, where Burleigh Street now is in the Strand